eBook and Digital Learning Tools

for

Democracy and the US Constitution

JOEL M. SIPRESS

Carefully scratch off the silver coating with a coin to see your personal redemption code.

Scratch here to reveal your access code. This access code may only be used by the original purchaser.

This code can be used only once and cannot be shared!

MW01078860

VIA THE OUP SITE

Visit **www.oup.com/us/ debatingamericanhistory**

⬇

Select the edition you are using and the student resources for that edition.

⬇

Click the link to upgrade your access to the student resources.

⬇

Follow the on-screen instructions.

Enter your personal redemption code when prompted on the checkout screen.

VIA YOUR SCHOOL'S LEARNING MANAGEMENT SYSTEM

Log in to your instructor's course.

⬇

When you click a link to a protected resource, you will be prompted to register for access.

⬇

Follow the on-screen instructions.

⬇

Enter your personal redemption code when prompted on the checkout screen.

For assistance with code redemption or registration, please contact customer support at **arc.support@oup.com**.

OXFORD
UNIVERSITY PRESS

PRAISE FOR *DEBATING AMERICAN HISTORY*

"*Debating American History* repositions the discipline of history as one that is rooted in discovery, investigation, and interpretation."
—Ingrid Dineen-Wimberly,
University of California, Santa Barbara

"*Debating American History* is an excellent replacement for a 'big assignment' in a course. Offering a way to add discussion to a class, it is also a perfect 'active learning' assignment, in a convenient package."
—Gene Rhea Tucker, Temple College

"The advantage that *Debating American History* has over other projects and texts currently available is that it brings a very clear and focused organization to the notion of classroom debate. The terms of each debate are clear. The books introduce students to historiography and primary sources. Most of all, the project re-envisions the way that US history should be taught. No other textbook or set of teaching materials does what these books do when taken together as the sum of their parts."
—Ian Hartman, University of Alaska

DEBATING AMERICAN HISTORY

DEMOCRACY AND THE US CONSTITUTION

DEBATING AMERICAN HISTORY

Series Editors: Joel M. Sipress, David J. Voelker

Conflict and Accommodation in Colonial New Mexico

The Powhatans and the English in the Seventeenth-Century Chesapeake

Democracy and the US Constitution

The Causes of the Civil War

Emancipation and the End of Slavery

Industrialization and Social Conflict in the Gilded Age

DEBATING AMERICAN HISTORY

DEMOCRACY AND THE US CONSTITUTION

Joel M. Sipress

UNIVERSITY OF WISCONSIN–SUPERIOR

NEW YORK   OXFORD
OXFORD UNIVERSITY PRESS

Oxford University Press is a department of the University of Oxford.
It furthers the University's objective of excellence in research, scholarship,
and education by publishing worldwide. Oxford is a registered trade mark of
Oxford University Press in the UK and certain other countries.

Published in the United States of America by Oxford University Press
198 Madison Avenue, New York, NY 10016, United States of America.

Library of Congress Cataloging-in-Publication Data
Names: Sipress, Joel M., author, compiler.
Title: Democracy and the U.S. Constitution / Joel M. Sipress, University of
    Wisconsin-Superior.
Other titles: Democracy and the United States Constitution.
Description: New York : Oxford University Press, 2020. | Series: Debating
    American history | Includes index.
Identifiers: LCCN 2018058942 | ISBN 9780190057091 (pbk.)
Subjects: LCSH: Constitutional history—United States—18th century—Sources.
    | United States—History—Study and teaching (Higher)
Classification: LCC KF4513 .S57 2020 | DDC 342.7302/909033—dc23 LC record available at
https://lccn.loc.gov/2018058942

Printing number: 9 8 7 6 5 4 3 2 1
Printed by LSC Communications, Inc., United States of America

TABLE OF CONTENTS

LIST OF TABLES   xi
ABOUT THE AUTHOR   xiii
ACKNOWLEDGMENTS   xv
SERIES INTRODUCTION   xvii

The Big Question   1

Timeline   9

Historians' Conversations   13

   Position #1—"We Hold These Truths to be Self-Evident": The Creation of
   a Democratic Republic   15

   Position #2—An Excess of Democracy: The Federalist Assault on Popular
   Self-Government   19

   Position #3—A Republic of Propertied Men: The Constitution in
   Historical Context   23

Debating the Question   27

   Declarations and Constitutions   29

      1.1 The Declaration of Independence (1776)
      1.2 The Articles of Confederation (1777)
      1.3 The Constitution of the United States (1787)
      1.4 The Constitutions of Virginia (1776) and Pennsylvania (1776)
      1.5 The Bill of Rights (1789)

Federalist Documents 63

2.1 Letter from Alexander Hamilton to James Duane (1780)

2.2 Alexander Hamilton, "Conjectures about the Constitution" (1787)

2.3 James Madison, "Vices of the Political System of the United States" (1787)

2.4 James Madison, "Federalist No. 10" (1787)

2.5 James Madison, "Federalist No. 51" (1788)

Documents from Shays' Rebellion 82

3.1 Daniel Gray, "An Address to the People of the Several Towns in the County of Hampshire, Now at Arms" (1786) and Thomas Grover, "To the Printer of the Hampshire Herald" (1786)

Anti-Federalist Documents 85

4.1 Essay by Montezuma (1787)

4.2 "Political Creed of Every Federalist" (1787)

4.3 Mercy Otis Warren, "Observations on the New Constitution, and on the Federal and State Conventions by a Columbian Patriot" (1788)

4.4 Virginia Convention Recommends Amendments to the Constitution (1788)

Voting Restrictions and Slave Laws in the Thirteen Original States 106

Biographies of Key Federalists 108

6.1 Alexander Hamilton

6.2 James Madison

ADDITIONAL RESOURCES 112

INDEX 113

LIST OF TABLES

Table 1   Voting Restrictions in the Thirteen Original States
Table 2   Slavery and Abolition in the Thirteen Original States

ABOUT THE AUTHOR

Joel M. Sipress received his PhD in United States history from the University of North Carolina at Chapel Hill. He is a Professor of History at the University of Wisconsin–Superior, where he teaches US and Latin American History. He has published articles and book chapters on the history of the US South with a focus on the role of race and class in late nineteenth-century southern politics. He has also written essays on teaching and learning history, including "Why Students Don't Get Evidence and What We Can Do About It," *The History Teacher* 37 (May 2004): 351–363; and "The End of the History Survey Course: The Rise and Fall of the Coverage Model," coauthored with David J. Voelker, *Journal of American History* 97 (March 2011): 1050–1066, which won the 2012 Maryellen Weimer Scholarly Work on Teaching and Learning Award. He serves as co-editor of *Debating American History* with David J. Voelker.

ACKNOWLEDGMENTS

We owe gratitude to Aeron Haynie, Regan Gurung, and Nancy Chick for introducing us and pairing us to work on the Signature Pedagogies project many years ago, as well as to the UW System's Office of Professional and Instructional Development (OPID), which supported that endeavor. Brian Wheel, formerly with Oxford University Press, helped us develop the idea for *Debating American History* and started the project rolling. We want to thank Charles Cavaliere at Oxford for taking on the project and seeing it through to publication, and Anna Russell for her excellent production work. Joel thanks the University of Wisconsin–Superior for support from a sabbatical, and David thanks the University of Wisconsin–Green Bay for support from a Research Scholar grant. David would also like to thank his colleagues in humanities, history, and First Nations Studies, who have been supportive of this project for many years, and Joel thanks his colleagues in the Department of Social Inquiry. We are also indebted to our colleagues (too numerous to mention) who have advanced the Scholarship of Teaching and Learning within the field of history. Without their efforts, this project would not have been possible. We would also like the thank the reviewers of this edition: Matthew J. Clavin, University of Houston; Amani Marshall, Georgia State University; Philip Levy, University of South Florida; Ingrid Dineen-Wimberly, U of Calif., Santa Barbara and U of La Verne; Kristin Hargrove, Grossmont College; Melanie Beals Goan, University of Kentucky; Paul Hart, Texas State University; Ross A. Kennedy, Illinois State University; Scott Laderman, University of Minnesota, Duluth; John Putnam, San Diego State University; Matt Tribbe, University of Houston; Linda Tomlinson, Fayetteville State University; Shauna Hann, United States Military Academy; Michael Holm, Boston University; Raymond J. Krohn, Boise State University; Joseph Locke, University of Houston-Victoria; Ted Moore, Salt Lake Community College; Andrew L. Slap, East Tennessee State University; Luke Harlow, University of Tennessee, Knoxville; Matthew Pinsker, Dickinson College; Tyina Steptoe, University of Arizona; Daniel Vivian, University of Louisville; Melanie Benson Taylor, Dartmouth College; Todd Romero, University of Houston; Robert J. Allison, Suffolk University, Boston; and, Joshua Fulton, Moraine Valley Community College.

SERIES INTRODUCTION

Although history instruction has grown richer and more varied over the past few decades, many college-level history teachers remain wedded to the coverage model, whose overriding design principle is to cover huge swaths of history, largely through the use of textbooks and lectures. The implied rationale supporting the coverage model is that students must be exposed to a wide array of facts, narratives, and concepts to have the necessary background both to be effective citizens and to study history at a more advanced level—something that few students actually undertake. Although coverage-based courses often afford the opportunity for students to encounter primary sources, the imperative to cover an expansive body of material dominates these courses; and the main assessment technique, whether implemented through objective or written exams, is to require students to identify or reproduce authorized knowledge.

Unfortunately, the coverage model has been falling short of its own goals since its very inception in the late nineteenth century. Educators and policymakers have been lamenting the historical ignorance of American youth going back to at least 1917, as Stanford professor of education Sam Wineburg documented in his illuminating exposé of the history of standardized tests of historical knowledge.[1] In 2010, the *New York Times* declared that "History is American students' worst subject," basing this judgment on yet another round of abysmal standardized test scores.[2] As we have documented in our own historical research, college professors over the past century have episodically criticized the coverage model and offered alternatives. Recently, however, college-level history instructors have been forming a scholarly community to improve the teaching of the introductory course by doing research that includes rigorous analysis of student learning. A number of historians who have become

---

1 Sam Wineburg, "Crazy for History," *Journal of American History* 90 (March 2004): 1401–1414.
2 Sam Dillon, "U.S. Students Remain Poor at History, Tests Show," *New York Times*, June 14, 2011. Accessed online at http://www.nytimes.com/2011/06/15/education/15history.html?emc=eta1&pagewanted=print.

involved in this discipline-based pedagogical research, known as the Scholarship of Teaching and Learning (SoTL), have begun to mount a challenge to the coverage model.[3]

Not only has the coverage model often achieved disappointing results by its own standards, it also proves ineffective at helping students learn how to think historically, which has long been a stated goal of history education. As Lendol Calder argued in a seminal 2006 article, the coverage model works to "cover up" or "conceal" the nature of historical thinking.[4] The eloquent lecture or the unified textbook narrative reinforces the idea that historical knowledge consists of a relatively straightforward description of the past. Typical methods of covering content hide from students not only the process of historical research—the discovery and interpretation of sources—but also the ongoing and evolving discussions among historians about historical meaning. In short, the coverage model impedes historical thinking by obscuring the fact that history is a complex, interpretative, and argumentative discourse.

Informed by the scholarship of the processes of teaching and learning, contemporary reformers have taken direct aim at the assumption that factual and conceptual knowledge must precede more sophisticated forms of historical study. Instead, reformers stress that students must learn to think historically by doing—at a novice level—what expert historians do.[5]

With these ideas in mind, we thus propose an argument-based model for teaching the introductory history course. In the argument-based model, students participate in a contested, evidence-based discourse about the human past. In other words, students are asked to argue about history. And by arguing, students develop the dispositions and habits of mind that are central to the discipline of history.[6] As the former American Historical Association (AHA) president Kenneth Pomeranz noted in late 2013, historians should consider seeing general education history courses as valuable "not for the sake of 'general

---

3   See Lendol Calder, "Uncoverage: Toward a Signature Pedagogy for the History Survey," *Journal of American History* 92 (March 2006): 1358–1370; Joel M. Sipress and David J. Voelker, "The End of the History Survey Course: The Rise and Fall of the Coverage Model," *Journal of American History* 97 (March 2011): 1050–1066; and Penne Restad, "American History Learned, Argued, and Agreed Upon," in Michael Sweet and Larry K. Michaelson, eds., *Team-Based Learning in the Social Sciences and Humanities*, 159–180 (Sterling, VA: Stylus, 2012). For an overview of the Scholarship of Teaching and Learning (SoTL) in history, see Joel M. Sipress and David Voelker, "From Learning History to Doing History: Beyond the Coverage Model," in *Exploring Signature Pedagogies: Approaches to Teaching Disciplinary Habits of Mind*, pp. 19–35, edited by Regan Gurung, Nancy Chick, and Aeron Haynie (Stylus Publishing, 2008). Note also that the International Society for the Scholarship of Teaching and Learning in History was formed in 2006. See http://www.indiana.edu/~histsotl/blog/.

4   Calder, "Uncoverage," 1362–1363.

5   For influential critiques of the "facts first" assumption, see Sam Wineburg, "Crazy for History," *Journal of American History* 90 (March 2004), 1401–1414; and Calder, "Uncoverage."

6   For discussions of argument-based courses, see Barbara E. Walvoord and John R. Breihan, "Arguing and Debating: Breihan's History Course," in Barbara E. Walvoord and Lucille P. McCarthy, *Thinking and Writing in College: A Naturalistic Study of Students in Four Disciplines* (Urbana, IL: National Council of Teachers of English, 1990), 97–143; Todd Estes, "Constructing the Syllabus: Devising a Framework for Helping Students Learn to Think Like Historians," *History Teacher* 40 (February 2007), 183–201; Joel M. Sipress, "Why Students Don't Get Evidence and What We Can Do About It," *The History Teacher* 37 (May 2004), 351–363; and David J. Voelker, "Assessing Student Understanding in Introductory Courses: A Sample Strategy," *The History Teacher* 41 (August 2008): 505–518.

knowledge' but for the intellectual operations you can teach."[7] Likewise, the AHA "Tuning Project" defines the discipline in a way much more consistent with an argument-based course than with the coverage model:

> History is a set of evolving rules and tools that allows us to interpret the past with clarity, rigor, and an appreciation for interpretative debate. It requires evidence, sophisticated use of information, and a deliberative stance to explain change and continuity over time. As a profoundly public pursuit, history is essential to active and empathetic citizenship and requires effective communication to make the past accessible to multiple audiences. As a discipline, history entails a set of professional ethics and standards that demand peer review, citation, and toleration for the provisional nature of knowledge."[8]

We have designed *Debating American History* with these values in mind.

In the coverage-based model, historical knowledge is seen as an end in itself. In the argument-based model, by contrast, the historical knowledge that students must master serves as a body of evidence to be employed in argument and debate. While the ultimate goal of the coverage approach is the development of a kind of cultural literacy, the argument-based history course seeks to develop historical modes of thinking and to encourage students to incorporate these modes of thinking into their daily lives. Particularly when housed within a broader curriculum that emphasizes engaged learning, an argument-based course prepares students to ask useful questions in the face of practical problems and challenges—whether personal, professional, or civic. On encountering a historical claim, such as those that frequently arise in political discussions, they will know how to ask important questions about context, evidence, and logic. In this way, the argument-based course fulfills the discipline's longstanding commitment to the cultivation of engaged and informed citizens.[9]

While there is no single correct way to structure an argument-based course, such courses do share a number of defining characteristics that drive course design.[10] In particular, argument-based courses include these elements:

1. THEY ARE ORGANIZED AROUND SIGNIFICANT HISTORICAL QUESTIONS ABOUT WHICH HISTORIANS THEMSELVES DISAGREE.

Argument-based courses are, first and foremost, question-driven courses in which "big" historical questions (rather than simply topics or themes) provide the overall organizational

---

7   Kenneth Pomeranz, "Advanced History for Beginners: Why We Should Bring What's Best about the Discipline into the Gen Ed Classroom," *Perspectives on History* (November 2013), at http://www.historians.org/publications-and-directories/perspectives-on-history/november-2013/advanced-history-for-beginners-why-we-should-bring-whats-best-about-the-discipline-into-the-gen-ed-classroom.

8   This definition reflects the state of the Tuning Project as of September 2013. For more information, see "AHA History Tuning Project: 2013 History Discipline Core," at https://www.historians.org/teaching-and-learning/tuning-the-history-discipline/2013-history-discipline-core. Accessed January 31, 2019.

9   As recently as 2006, the AHA's Teaching Division reasserted the importance of history study and scholarship in the development of globally aware citizens. Patrick Manning, "Presenting History to Policy Makers: Three Position Papers," *Perspectives: The Newsmagazine of the American Historical Association* 44 (March 2006), 22–24.

10 Our approach to course design is deeply influenced by Grant Wiggins and Jay McTighe, *Understanding by Design*, 2nd ed. (Upper Saddle River, NJ: Pearson Education, 2006).

structure. A "big" historical question is one about which historians themselves disagree and that has broad academic, intellectual, or cultural implications. Within these very broad parameters, the types of questions around which a course may be organized can vary greatly. The number of "big" questions addressed, however, must be relatively limited in number (perhaps three to five over the course of a typical fifteen-week semester), so that students can pursue the questions in depth.

2. THEY SYSTEMATICALLY EXPOSE STUDENTS TO RIVAL POSITIONS ABOUT WHICH THEY MUST MAKE INFORMED JUDGMENTS.

Argument-based courses systematically expose students to rival positions about which they must form judgments. Through repeated exploration of rival positions on a series of big questions, students see historical debate modeled in way that shatters any expectation that historical knowledge is clear-cut and revealed by authority. Students are thus confronted with the inescapable necessity to engage, consider, and ultimately evaluate the merits of a variety of perspectives.

3. THEY ASK STUDENTS TO JUDGE THE RELATIVE MERITS OF RIVAL POSITIONS ON BASIS OF HISTORICAL EVIDENCE.

To participate in historical argument, students must understand historical argument as more than a matter of mere opinion. For this to happen, students must learn to employ evidence as the basis for evaluating historical claims. Through being repeatedly asked to judge the relative merits of rival positions on the basis of evidence, students learn to see the relationship between historical evidence and historical assertions.

4. THEY REQUIRE STUDENTS TO DEVELOP THEIR OWN POSITIONS FOR WHICH THEY MUST ARGUE ON THE BASIS OF HISTORICAL EVIDENCE.

In an argument-based course, the ultimate aspiration should be for students to bring their own voices to bear on historical discourse in a way that is thoroughly grounded in evidence. Students must therefore have the opportunity to argue for their own positions. Such positions may parallel or synthesize those of the scholars with which they have engaged in the course or they may be original. In either case, though, students must practice applying disciplinary standards of evidence.

Learning to argue about history is, above all, a process that requires students to develop new skills, dispositions, and habits of mind. Students develop these attributes through the act of arguing in a supportive environment where the instructor provides guidance and feedback. The instructor is also responsible for providing students with the background, context, and in-depth materials necessary both to fully understand and appreciate each big question and to serve as the body of evidence that forms the basis for judgments and arguments. While argument-based courses eschew any attempt to provide comprehensive coverage, they ask students to think deeply about a smaller number of historical questions—and in the process of arguing about the selected questions, students will develop significant content knowledge in the areas emphasized.

While a number of textbooks and readers in American history incorporate elements of historical argumentation, there are no published materials available that are specifically designed to support an argument-based course. *Debating American History* consists of a series of modular units, each focused on a specific topic and question in American history that will support all four characteristics of an argument-based course noted previously. Instructors will select units that support their overall course design, perhaps incorporating one or two modules into an existing course or structuring an entire course around three to five such units. (Instructors, of course, are free to supplement the modular units with other materials of their choosing, such as additional primary documents, secondary articles, multimedia materials, and book chapters.) By focusing on a limited number of topics, students will be able to engage in in-depth historical argumentation, including consideration of multiple positions and substantial bodies of evidence.

Each unit has the following elements:

1. THE BIG QUESTION

A brief narrative introduction that poses the central question of the unit and provides general background.

2. HISTORIANS' CONVERSATIONS

This section establishes the debate by providing two or three original essays that present distinct and competing scholarly positions on the Big Question. While these essays make occasional reference to major scholars in the field, they are not intended to provide historiographical overviews but rather to provide models of historical argumentation through the presentation and analysis of evidence.

3. DEBATING THE QUESTION

Each module includes a variety of materials containing evidence for students to use to evaluate the various positions and develop a position of their own. Materials may include primary source documents, images, a timeline, maps, or brief secondary sources. The specific materials vary depending on the nature of the question. Some modules include detailed case studies that focus on a particular facet of the Big Question.

For example, one module that we have developed for an early American history course focuses on the following Big Question: "How were the English able to displace the thriving Powhatan people from their Chesapeake homelands in the seventeenth century?" The Historians' Conversations section includes two essays: "Position #1: The Overwhelming Advantages of the English"; and "Position #2: Strategic Mistakes of the Powhatans." The unit materials allow students to undertake a guided exploration of both Powhatan and English motivations and strategies. The materials include two case studies that serve specific pedagogical purposes. The first case study asks the question, "Did Pocahontas Rescue John Smith from Execution?" Answering this question requires grappling with the nature of primary sources and weighing additional evidence from secondary sources; given historians' confidence that Powhatan did adopt Smith during his captivity, the case study also raises important questions about Powhatan strategy. The second case study focuses on the 1622 surprise attack that the Powhatans (led by Opechancanough) launched against the English, posing the question, "What Was the Strategy behind the 1622 Powhatan Surprise Attack?" Students wrestle with a number of scholarly perspectives regarding Opechancanough's purpose and the effectiveness of his strategy. Overall, this unit introduces students to the use of primary sources and the process of weighing different historical interpretations. Because of Disney's 1995 film *Pocahontas*, many students begin the unit thinking that they already know about the contact between the Powhatans and the English; many of them also savor the chance to bring critical, historical thinking to bear on this subject, and doing so deepens their understanding of how American Indians responded to European colonization.

Along similar lines, the Big Question for a module on the Gilded Age asks, "Why Was Industrialization in the Late Nineteenth Century Accompanied by Such Great Social and Political Turmoil?" The materials provided allow students to explore the labor conflicts of the period as well as the Populist revolt and to draw conclusions regarding the underlying causes of the social and political upheavals. Primary sources allow students to delve into labor conflicts from the perspectives of both workers and management and to explore both Populist and anti-Populist perspectives. Three short case studies allow students to examine specific instances of social conflict in depth. A body of economic data from the late nineteenth century is also included.

Many history instructors, when presented with the argument-based model, find its goals to be compelling, but they fear that it is overly ambitious—that introductory-level students will be incapable of engaging in historical thinking at an acceptable level. But, we must ask, how well do students learn under the coverage model? Student performance varies in an argument-based course, but it varies widely in a coverage-based course as well. In our experience, most undergraduate students are capable of achieving a basic-level competence at identifying and evaluating historical interpretations and using primary and secondary sources as evidence to make basic historical arguments. We not only have evidence of this success in the form of our own grade books, but we have studied our students' learning to document the success of our approach.[11] Students can indeed learn how to think like historians at a novice level, and in doing so they will gain both an appreciation for the discipline and develop a set of critical skills and dispositions that will contribute to their overall higher education. For this to happen, however, a course must be "backward designed" to promote and develop historical thinking. As historian Lawrence Gipson (Wabash College) asked in a 1916 AHA discussion, "Will the student catch 'historical-mindedness' from his instructor like the mumps?"[12] The answer, clearly, is "no."

In addition to the modular units focused on big questions, instructors will also be provided with a brief instructors' manual, entitled "Developing an Argument-Based Course." This volume will provide instructors with guidance and advice on course development, as well as with sample in-class exercises and assessments. Additionally, each module includes

---

11 See Sipress, "Why Students Don't Get Evidence," and Voelker, "Assessing Student Understanding."

12 Lawrence H. Gipson, "Method of the Elementary Course in the Small College," *The History Teacher's Magazine* 8 (April 1917), 128. (The conference discussion took place in 1916.)

an Instructor's Manual. Together, these resources will assist instructors with the process of creating an argument-based course, whether for a relatively small class at a liberal arts college or for a large class of students at a university. These resources can be used in both face-to-face and online courses.

The purpose of *Debating American History* is to provide instructors with both the resources and strategies that they will need to design such a course. This textbook alternative leaves plenty of room for instructor flexibility; and it requires instructors to carefully choose, organize, and introduce the readings to students, as well as to coach students through the process of thinking historically, even as they deepen their knowledge and understanding of particular eras and topics.

Joel M. Sipress
Professor of History,
University of Wisconsin-Superior

David J. Voelker
Associate Professor of Humanities and History,
University of Wisconsin-Green Bay

DEBATING AMERICAN HISTORY

DEMOCRACY AND THE US CONSTITUTION

THE BIG QUESTION

HOW DEMOCRATIC WAS THE US CONSTITUTION?

In late May of 1787, twenty-nine delegates from nine of the thirteen states gathered in the city of Philadelphia to draft proposed amendments to the Articles of Confederation, the governing document of the newly independent United States of America. Over the course of the summer, a total fifty-five delegates came to Philadelphia, with all the states except Rhode Island represented. Among those present were such luminaries of the American Revolution as George Washington (commander of the Continental Army) and a number of signatories of the Declaration of Independence, including Benjamin Franklin, Roger Sherman, Robert Morris, Elbridge Gerry, and George Wythe.

The delegates to the convention were united by their concerns that the Articles of Confederation had left the federal government without the powers necessary to fulfill its most basic functions. Adopted in the midst of the Revolutionary War, the Articles of Confederation reflected the revolutionaries' fears that a powerful central government that was distant from the people would abuse its powers, much as they believed that the British government had done in the years leading up to the Revolution. The Articles envisioned a loose confederation of sovereign states bound together primarily for purposes of mutual defense and cooperation. The Articles established a Congress made up of delegates from the thirteen states in which each state received a single vote. The authority of the Congress, however, was quite limited (excluding, for instance, the power to regulate trade or to raise tax revenues directly from the people); and the exercise of its most important powers (such as the power to spend or borrow money) required the support of nine of the thirteen state delegations. The Articles allowed the Congress to establish departments to conduct the day-to-day business of the government, but they contained no provision for a chief executive (like a president) to oversee the operations of these departments. Under the Articles, each state retained important powers, such as the authority to issue its own money and to impose duties (taxes) on goods imported or exported through its ports. Congress remained dependent on financial contributions from the individual states to fund government operations but lacked any mechanism to compel states to pay the moneys owed.

Almost immediately upon the ratification of the Articles of Confederation in 1781, its weaknesses became apparent. The Congress had accumulated massive debts to finance the Revolutionary War, and without any reliable source of revenue, these debts went largely unpaid—rendering the money issued by the Congress virtually worthless. (For a generation, "good as a Continental" remained American slang for something of little value.) Meanwhile, the British had barred American ships from its colonies in the Caribbean, thus depriving the new nation's merchants of the profits of this lucrative trade. Lacking the authority to establish a uniform trade policy for the individual states, the federal government could do little to force the British to reopen their ports. Even the very territorial integrity of the newly independent United States appeared at risk, as the British refused to withdraw their military outposts from the country's northwestern territories, as required under the treaty that had ended the Revolution. The United States faced a growing number of threats from a variety of European powers, and the central government established under the Articles lacked the ability to respond effectively.

During the 1780s, repeated efforts were made to amend the Articles of Confederation to grant the federal Congress additional authority. The Articles' requirement that amendments must be approved unanimously by the legislatures of all thirteen states, however, proved to be an insurmountable obstacle. In September 1786, representatives from five states gathered in Annapolis, Maryland, to discuss the commercial and trade problems the country faced. Among those present was Alexander Hamilton of New York, a thirty-year-old Revolutionary War veteran who had served as chief of staff to George Washington. From humble beginnings, Hamilton had risen to become of major figure in New York's political and financial circles, a status cemented by his marriage to Elizabeth Schuyler, a member of one of the state's most prominent families. At Hamilton's instigation, the Annapolis convention issued a call for a second gathering at Philadelphia for the following May to draft proposed amendments to the Articles of Confederation. Seeking the greatest possible legitimacy for the Philadelphia convention, Hamilton and his allies asked the federal Congress to support the gathering. In February 1787, a reluctant Congress endorsed the Philadelphia convention "for the sole and express purpose of revising the Articles of Confederation."[1]

Although support for strengthening the powers of the Congress under the Articles was widespread within the states, Hamilton and his allies (including Virginia's James Madison) had a broader agenda. Hamilton and Madison, concerned by the direction politics had taken within the individual states, envisioned a radical shift in authority to the central government that would strip the states of many of the powers they enjoyed under the Articles. Prior the American Revolution, colonial politics had been a sedate affair in which a relatively small group of well-educated and well-connected men had taken on political leadership roles. During the Revolution, however, men of more modest means, such as farmers and artisans, became more active in politics and government. (Women, of course, lacked the right to vote, as did the propertyless and the enslaved.) In some cases, these men of modest means had pushed traditional political leaders aside and pursued policies that such leaders considered irresponsible. Hamilton and Madison saw the Philadelphia convention as a chance not simply to augment the powers of the Congress but also to rein in what they saw as the excesses of the states.

Especially controversial were policies pursued at the state level to relieve the debt burdens of hard-pressed farmers. The disruptions of war and a harsh economic depression

---

1   Rough Journals of the Congress, February 21, 1787, in Merrill Jensen, ed., *The Documentary History of the Ratification of the Constitution*, vol. 1 (Madison: State Historical Society of Wisconsin, 1976), 187.

that followed had left many small farmers owing large sums of money to merchants. Flexing their new-found political muscles, indebted farmers in a number of states elected their own representatives to office and pushed through legislation intended to reduce the burden of debt. The most common debt relief measure was to increase the amount of money in circulation through the printing of paper currency. An increase in the amount of money in circulation would assist debtors in a simple yet ingenious way. An increase in the money supply reduces the value of money relative to goods, such as the goods that farmers produced. Or, to put it otherwise, farmers would receive more money for the goods they sold, making it easier to pay off their debts. Of course, they would pay back their debts in money whose value had gone down, which naturally aroused the ire of the merchants to whom they owed the money. The explosive potential of the debt issue was illustrated vividly in Rhode Island where, in 1786, the state legislature (dominated by representatives of indebted farmers) issued vast quantities of paper money. Many merchants shut their doors to avoid being paid in what they considered worthless money; and others fled the state entirely, leaving many in Rhode Island's urban areas without access to the basic necessities of life. In the city of Newport, members of the urban lower classes stormed the local merchant houses to gain access to stores of corn and wheat.

The turmoil in Rhode Island was soon overshadowed by armed rebellion in neighboring Massachusetts. Like the indebted farmers of Rhode Island, those in Massachusetts had lobbied their legislature for an increase in the supply of money through the printing of money. Farmers also protested high taxes, the proceeds of which went largely to pay off debts owed to the wealthy merchants in Boston who had lent the state government money to finance the Revolutionary War. When the state legislature rejected these demands, a group of farmers in the western part of the state, led by a Revolutionary War veteran named Daniel Shays, rose up in arms. The rebellion began in the fall of 1786 with armed groups shutting down local courts to prevent foreclosure procedures against indebted farmers. In January 1787, a group of roughly 1,200 rebels seeking arms and ammunition attacked a federal arsenal in the town of Springfield. The attack was repulsed by a contingent of state militia, and the rebellion shortly thereafter collapsed. Nonetheless, Shays' Rebellion sent shock waves through the political elite of the thirteen states. George Washington, for instance, wrote, "There are combustibles in every State which a spark might set fire to."[2] For leaders like Hamilton and Madison, events in Rhode Island and Massachusetts epitomized the dangers of what they saw as local politics run amuck and raised fears that the republic itself might be engulfed in anarchy.

The Philadelphia convention met in the shadow of Shays' Rebellion. Madison and Hamilton (both of whom were delegates) had already concluded that a radical shift in power to the central government was required to bring an end to the disorders in the states, and they acted swiftly to move the other delegates in their direction. Prior to the start of the convention, Madison had drafted a proposal to scrap the Articles of Confederation in its entirety and replace it with a new constitution in which the supremacy of the federal government would be clearly established. Madison's proposal called for a

---

2   George Brown Tindall and David E. Shi, *America: A Narrative History*, 4th ed. (New York: W.W. Norton, 1996), 298.

restructured federal Congress with augmented powers, a president who would act as a chief executive officer, and a system of federal courts. States would be stripped of many of their powers, particularly over matters of economics and trade. Madison also proposed bypassing the amendment process outlined in the Articles (which required unanimity of all 13 state legislatures to make a change) in favor of another, as of yet unspecified, ratification process. Presented to the delegates as the "Virginia Plan," Madison's proposal was, strictly speaking, a call to revolution, as the Philadelphia Convention lacked any legal basis to dispense with the Articles of Confederation and its system of government.

Although many delegates took issue with aspects of Madison's proposal, the Virginia Plan nonetheless established the framework for the convention's deliberations. Working in secret over the summer of 1787, the delegates addressed a series of difficult issues, including the method of election for the various government branches and the apportionment of congressional representatives among the several states. The delegates also agreed to a method for ratification of their work. Bypassing the state legislatures (who were likely to resist a proposal that stripped them of much of their authority), each state would be asked to call a specially elected convention to approve or reject the document. Ignoring the Articles' requirement for unanimity, the proposed constitution would go into effect when nine of the thirteen states had granted their approval. (It would only be binding on those states that ratified it.) In a gesture to Articles of Confederation, the convention submitted its work to the existing Congress for approval and transmission to the states for ratification.

From the moment in September of 1787 when the convention adjourned and made its work public, the proposed constitution became the subject of a passionate and spirited debate. Advocates of the proposal argued that it struck the proper balance between democratic representation, centralized authority, and protections against the abuse of government power. Critics, by contrast, declared the proposed constitution to be an "aristocratic" document that stripped the common man of his power and shifted authority to an elite of the wealthy and well connected. Skeptics found the absence of a Bill of Rights, which would place specific limits on the power of the central government by defining inviolable rights of the people, to be particularly worrisome. Although Delaware, Pennsylvania, New Jersey, Georgia, and Connecticut quickly ratified the document, its ultimate fate remained unclear, as well-organized opposition emerged in the other states. In a concession to opponents, the advocates of the constitution (who had taken the name "Federalists") promised that, should the document be ratified, they would support adding a Bill of Rights via the amendment process.

A turning point came in February of 1788 when the Federalists overcame strong resistance in Massachusetts to secure ratification in that state. Maryland and South Carolina followed suit, leaving New Hampshire as the ninth and deciding state. Opposition in that state was fierce, with its ratification convention having met on and off for months without coming to a decision. In June, though, New Hampshire's Federalists launched an all-out push to secure ratification making use of virtually every tactic and strategy they could employ, including (according to local lore) treating a group of anti-Federalist delegates to a drunken luncheon on the day of the final vote to ensure their absence when the final ballots were cast. On June 21, 1788, by a narrow margin of 57–47 votes, New Hampshire gave its approval: and the United States Constitution was declared to be officially ratified. After spirited battles, two of the largest states (Virginia and New York) narrowly gave their approval shortly thereafter. North Carolina and Rhode Island continued to resist for a time; but by 1791, all thirteen states had ratified the document and were full participating members of the newly strengthened union. Keeping their promise to opponents of the Constitution, Federalists (led by James Madison) helped to draft and ratify a Bill of Rights comprised of ten constitutional amendments that defined a series of individual rights that the newly established federal government was barred from violating.

Over time, the US Constitution came to be seen as a founding document of American democracy—a document that lay the foundation for a political system that empowered Americans to govern their own affairs as free and equal citizens. For the first century following the document's ratification, the objections of the anti-Federalists and their claims that the Constitution was an "aristocratic" document that enshrined the rule of the wealthy and well-born were largely forgotten. In 1913, however, historian Charles Beard (a faculty member at Columbia University) published *An Economic Interpretation of the Constitution of the United States* in which he argued that the Constitution was actually an anti-democratic document crafted by representatives of the new nation's commercial elites for the purpose of empowering themselves at the expense of the common people. Although Beard's argument initially faced a hostile reception, by the 1930s, many historians had embraced his position, setting up a scholarly debate among historians that continues to this day. To what extent *did* the Constitution establish a system of government that allowed the people of the newly independent United States to govern themselves on the basis of equality? To what extent did the Constitution limit the political power of ordinary people for the benefit of the wealthy and well connected? How democratic was the United States Constitution?

TIMELINE

1775

Fighting breaks out between British troops and patriot militia in the Boston area. Fighting spreads to other colonies.

1776

The Second Continental Congress declares the thirteen colonies to be independent of Great Britain. The Declaration of Independence is issued.

1776–1780

Each of the thirteen former colonies adopts a state constitution delineating the structure, powers, and limits of the state's government.

1777

Congress adopts proposed Articles of Confederation and sends them to the states for ratification.

1781

The last of the thirteen states ratify the Articles of Confederation and the document is adopted.

1781

Surrender of British forces at Yorktown, Virginia brings the Revolutionary War essentially to an end.

1781–1786

Failed attempts to amend the Articles of Confederation to grant additional powers to the central government.

1783

Treaty of Paris signed. Revolutionary War officially ends. Great Britain recognizes the independence of the former colonies.

1785–86

Seven of the thirteen states issue paper money to provide financial relief to indebted farmers.

1786

Riots in Rhode Island when merchants cease business to prevent debts from being settled with paper money.

1786 (September)
Delegates from five states gather at Annapolis, Maryland, and issue a call for a convention to be held the following year at Philadelphia to draft proposed amendments to the Articles of Confederation.

1786 (August)–1787 (February)
Indebted farmers in western Massachusetts led by Revolutionary War veteran Daniel Shays rise in rebellion against the state government.

1787 (February)
Congress endorses the proposed Philadelphia convention "for the sole and express purpose of revising the Articles of Confederation."

1787 (May)
Delegates gather at Philadelphia for the convention. Delegates meet throughout the summer. Convention proceedings are kept secret.

1787 (September)
Convention completes its work and makes public its proposal to scrap the Articles of Confederation and replace it with radically different structure for the central government. The Convention proposes that the Articles amendment process be bypassed and that the proposed constitution go into effect when nine states, through specially elected ratification conventions, approve the document.

1787 (September)
Congress submits the proposed constitution to the states for ratification.

1787–1788
Eleven of the thirteen states ratify the proposed constitution. The Constitution of the United States is declared adopted.

1789–90
The two holdout states (North Carolina and Rhode Island) ratify the Constitution.

1789
Congress approves a set of proposed constitutional amendments to establish a federal Bill of Rights. Proposed amendments are sent to the states for ratification.

1791
The ten constitutional amendments comprising the Bill of Rights are ratified.

HISTORIANS' CONVERSATIONS

POSITION #1—"WE HOLD THESE TRUTHS TO BE SELF-EVIDENT"

The Creation of a Democratic Republic

Over a number of years, the colonists had become increasingly frustrated with the policies of the British Empire. It was simply wrong, they believed, to be subjected to imperial taxation when they had no voice whatsoever in the British Parliament. "Taxation without representation is tyranny," became their rallying cry. Colonists resisted through protests, boycotts, petitions, and ultimately through riots and mob action—culminating in the destruction of three entire shiploads of British tea in the famous Boston Tea Party of 1773. Fighting erupted between colonists and British soldiers just outside Boston in the spring of 1775, and the conflict soon spread across the thirteen colonies. By 1776, patriots (as the rebels called themselves) had come to realize that more was at stake in this war than just the issue of taxation. What was, in fact, at stake was an important principle—the principle that people have the right to govern themselves and be free from the whims of arbitrary authority. These principles were best summed up in Thomas Jefferson's famed Declaration of Independence. "We hold these truths to be self-evident," wrote Jefferson, "that all men are created equal, that they are endowed by their Creator with certain unalienable Rights, that among these are Life, Liberty and the pursuit of Happiness.—That to secure these rights, Governments are instituted among Men, deriving their just powers from the consent of the governed."

The British recognized the independence of the United States in the Treaty of Paris of 1783, which brought the Revolutionary War to an end. The work of the Revolution, however, was not yet complete. What remained to be done was to construct a national government based on the principles for which the revolutionaries had fought. It was that work that gave birth to the United States Constitution.

Having suffered under the policies of the British Empire, Americans were highly suspicious of centralized government. What is more, political philosophers had long warned that republican government (i.e., government by the people) could only thrive in relatively small nations. For these reasons, the revolutionaries originally envisioned the United States as a loose confederation of sovereign states with most political power located at the state level. By the late 1780s, however, it was broadly recognized that a stronger national government was required. Under the Articles of Confederation, the Congress lacked the ability to perform its most basic functions. Under the Articles, for instance, the Congress had no authority to regulate interstate trade. The result was a hodgepodge of trade regulations enacted by the individual states that undermined efforts to promote domestic manufacturing and commerce at a national level. Congress also lacked the ability to raise its own revenue, depriving the national government of the political and military strength to defend the interests of the United States in an Atlantic world still dominated by the empires of Western Europe. When rebels in western Massachusetts led by Daniel Shays rose up in arms in the fall of 1786, the government of the state was left to fend for itself, while leaders at the national level stood by helplessly. In the absence of a central government with the authority to effectively govern the nation, the newly independent United States faced the prospect of social, political, and economic anarchy.

The great challenge was to provide the central government with the powers it required without that government itself becoming a new kind of tyranny. The primary task of the delegates to the Constitutional Convention was thus to reconcile the need for a more powerful central government with the principles of liberty and democratic self-rule that the revolution had been fought for. Over the course of the summer of 1787, the delegates to the convention struggled to balance these two goals. In the end, they crafted a constitution that incorporated a number of important protections for the rights of the people. The most important of these safeguards was the division of the powers of the federal government into separate and distinct branches, each of which would act as a check and balance on the others. The separation of the government into distinct and independent branches would prevent any one individual, or a small group of individuals, from accumulating and exercising tyrannical power. The authority to enact laws, raise taxes, and appropriate funds was lodged in a legislative branch (known as the Congress) that was itself divided into two houses (the House of Representatives and the Senate) as an added protection. Administration of the daily affairs of the government, including command of the armed forces, was given to the President. The authority of the President was limited, though, by a series of additional powers (such as the power to declare war) that were granted to the Congress. Similarly, the powers of Congress were limited by the presidential veto over legislation. Finally, the power to interpret the law and apply it so specific cases was lodged in an independent judicial branch, whose judges were appointed for life by the President (with the approval of the Senate) to shield them from the corrupting influence of day-to-day politics.

To ensure that legislation would reflect the will of the people, the members of the House of Representatives were directly elected by the voters of each state and served for just two-year terms, subjecting them to regular accountability at the hands of the people. To provide stability, the President and members of the Senate served longer terms (four years and six years, respectively). The founders did have fears that unscrupulous politicians might manipulate the public to pursue ends that were damaging to the nation. The President and members of the Senate were, therefore, shielded to some extent from public opinion. Each state's senators were chosen by that state's legislature rather directly by the voters. (Members of the state legislatures were, of course, elected by voters.) The President was to be elected by an "electoral college" made up of representatives of each state. Each state's electors would be chosen in a manner to be determined by the state legislature. Finally, the constitution included a process for amendment so that it could be modified, should the people decide that this was necessary.

The delegates to the convention envisioned a central government that drew its authority directly from the people rather than from the various states. For that reason, they submitted their work directly to the voters of each state, who would express their will through specially elected ratification conventions. It is true that Federalists and anti-Federalists fought bitter battles over the issue of ratification. As historian Edmund Morgan writes, however, "the differences between Federalists and anti-Federalists were primarily differences about means, not fundamental differences of principle."[1] Many anti-Federalists understood that a more effective national government was needed, and both camps were committed to a republican form of government—a government of the people. Anti-Federalists, though, were concerned that the proposed constitution lacked sufficient safeguards for the rights of the people, and they were unwilling to shift power from the states to the federal government in the absence of such safeguards. "Opponents of the Constitution held to the old view," explains political scientist Martin Diamond, "that political power had to be tied down close to home. Its supporters urged the new view that great power could safely (if carefully) be assigned to the government of an extended republic."[2] Anti-Federalists were particularly concerned by the absence of a bill of rights that placed explicit limits on the powers of the central government. Federalists responded to this criticism by pledging that should the constitution be adopted, they would work to rapidly add a bill of rights via the constitutional amendment process. In fact, it was James Madison, the chief architect of the United States Constitution, who ushered the Bill of Rights through the amendment process during the inaugural session of the newly established federal Congress.

The United States Constitution was, by no means, a perfect reflection of the principles of liberty and self-government for which the revolutionaries had fought. The founding fathers were very much shaped by the prejudices of the culture of which they were a part, and these prejudices placed limits on their ability to act fully on their principles. Legislative appointment of US Senators and the electoral college system for selecting the President, for instance, rankle modern democratic sensibilities. (Direct election of US Senators was established by the 17th Amendment to the Constitution, ratified in 1912.) Similarly, the Constitution's implicit recognition of the institution of slavery stands at odds with the bold proclamation of the principle of human equality found in the Declaration of Independence. The Constitution, as well, was utterly silent on the matter of who could or could not vote, leaving that issue up to each individual state. For decades and even generations to come, particular states would maintain gender-, race-, and property-based restrictions on the right to vote. Not until 1919 was the Constitution amended to bar states from depriving individuals of the right to vote on the basis of sex. A number of states kept laws on the books that effectively deprived African American people of the right to vote all the way into the 1960s.

Yet, despite these limitations, the architects of the Constitution had gone far toward achieving the goals of the American Revolution. In the words of William A. Schambra "the Founders had been remarkably successful at bringing to life a kind of political

1   Edmund S. Morgan, *The Birth of the Republic, 1763–1789* (Chicago: University of Chicago Press, 1956), 155.
2   Martin Diamond, *The Founding of the Democratic Republic* (Itasca, IL: F.E. Peacock Publishers, 1981), 55.

order that hitherto they had only been able to admire in the writings of certain political philosophers."[3] The US Constitution put in place the basic framework for a system of government based on the principles of democratic self-rule and individual liberty. The work of building a fully democratic republic would be left to future generations, and it is work that continues to this day. Nevertheless, as Richard Beeman writes, "our Constitution has not only proven to be the world's most durable written frame of government, but it is also, I believe, its most just and equitable."[4]

---

3   Ibid. v.
4   Richard Beeman, *Plain and Honest Men: The Making of the American Constitution* (New York: Random House, 2009), xiii.

POSITION #2—AN EXCESS
OF DEMOCRACY
The Federalist Assault on Popular Self-Government

The American Revolution began as protest movement against the policies of the British Empire. Eventually it escalated into a war for independence. As historian Gordon Wood points out, though, the Revolution also unleashed powerful democratic forces *within* the thirteen colonies, as men of humble means came to see themselves as having both the right and the responsibility to help govern the affairs of their local communities and of the broader nation.[1] No one spoke more clearly for the democratic aspirations of the American Revolution than did Thomas Paine, whose 1776 pamphlet *Common Sense* tied the call for independence to a passionate critique of monarchy and aristocracy in all its forms. Similar themes animated Thomas Jefferson's Declaration of Independence, with its bold declaration that "all men are created equal."

In the wake of independence, however, the new nation's commercial and landowning elites came to fear that the Revolution's democratic tendencies had perhaps gone too far. In state after state, ordinary farmers and mechanics (as skilled craftsmen were called at the time), often led by Revolutionary War veterans, organized themselves politically and displaced the traditional governing class from their positions of prominence. New state constitutions were adopted that placed unprecedented power in the hands of democratically elected assemblies. Spurning the traditional political class, farmers and mechanics elected members of their own ranks to office and pursued policies that threatened the interests of wealthy merchants and creditors. In response, representatives of the elite (led by James Madison and Alexander Hamilton) launched a campaign to shift authority from the individual states to the central government, where they believed policymakers would be better shielded from what they saw as the corrupting influence of popular opinion. This movement culminated in the drafting of the United States Constitution, a document that placed significant restrictions on the democratic forces unleashed by the Revolution. As political scientist Michael Parenti writes, "the intent of the framers of the Constitution was to *contain* democracy, rather than give it free rein, and dilute the democratic will, rather than mobilize it."[2]

---

1 Gordon S. Wood, *The Radicalism of the American Revolution* (New York: Alfred A. Knopf, 1992), 3–8.
2 Michael Parenti, "The Constitution as an Elitist Document," in *How Democratic Is the Constitution?*, eds. Robert A. Goldwin and William A. Schambra (Washington, DC: American Enterprise Institute for Public Policy Research, 1980), 39.

By the standards of Europe, much of which was still dominated by an inherited aristocracy, the thirteen British colonies in North America were relatively egalitarian societies. Colonies like New York did have their large landowners with their European-style estates; and the southern colonies, of course, had developed slave-based plantation economies. Nonetheless, property in British North America was more widely held than in England, with small landowning farm households comprising the majority of the population in most colonies. When it came to matters of politics and government, though, the colonies replicated many of the aristocratic features of England. Connecticut and Rhode Island were the only two colonies to have elected governors. Elsewhere, the governor was appointed, either by the Crown or by the proprietor—the individual or business enterprise to whom the King had provided a colonial charter. Colonial governors had enormous powers, including the authority to appoint virtually every colonial official and local officials (with the exception of New England) as well. These appointments went overwhelmingly to well-connected merchants and larger landowners. Each colony did have an elected assembly; but the powers of these assemblies were modest, and the right to vote was limited by property restrictions. Those who could vote for assembly representatives tended to defer to their social "betters."

The American Revolution broke the back of the political aristocracy and brought ordinary men into the world of politics in unprecedented ways. The earliest protests against British taxation were organized by prominent citizens in port cities like Boston and Philadelphia. Over time, though, ordinary city dwellers, particular the skilled artisans, demanded representation and leadership roles on protest committees. As the protests spread to the countryside and began take the form of armed resistance, the farm population became central to the revolutionary movement, both as members of local militia companies and as enlistees in the Continental Army, the full-time revolutionary military force organized and led by General George Washington. Having fought a successful war for independence, these veterans returned home with new-found confidence and an unwillingness to defer to pre-war elites, even those who had sided with and helped to lead the struggle against Britain.

The democratic forces unleashed by the Revolution helped shape the new state constitutions drafted by the revolutionaries. In May of 1776 (a year into the war, but two months before independence was declared), the Continental Congress advised each colony to form new governments "under the authority of the people" and to totally suppress all vestiges of the authority of the British Crown.[3] Within these constitutions, the appointed governor positions were abolished, and the elected governors who replaced them were stripped of many of their powers, which were transferred to popularly elected state assemblies. Property restrictions for voting and holding office were lowered in many states and, in the case of Pennsylvania, were abolished entirely, though a requirement that voting be limited to taxpayers remained. Most states adopted formal declarations of rights, which specified in writing a list of specific liberties that the government of the state must hold inviolable. The backgrounds of those elected to serve in the various state assemblies also reflected the democratization of politics. In 1765, for instance,

---

3   Gordon S. Wood, *The American Revolution: A History* (New York: The Modern Library, 2002), 65.

wealthy gentlemen had comprised the bulk of New Hampshire's colonial assembly. By 1785, ordinary farmers and men of modest means made up the majority of the state's House of Representatives.[4]

The rise of commoners to positions of political prominence caused unease among the country's traditional governing class, and that unease only increased when some of the state assemblies began to pursue policies at odds with the interests of economic elites. The 1780s saw enormous hardship for many of the new nation's farmers who in some cases began to flex their new-found political muscles to advance their own interests. Economic dislocations caused by eight long years of war left many farmers in debt—a situation made worse by the removal of the United States from the British imperial trade system, which deprived farmers of access to overseas markets for their products. By 1786, seven of the thirteen states passed measures to relieve agricultural debt, with the most popular approach being the issuing of large sums of paper money to reduce the value of the currency and make it easier for farmers to earn the sums needed to pay off creditors. Understandably, the merchants who had loaned farmers money were appalled to discover that they would be paid back in what they considered worthless money. For many among the country's economic and political elite, the paper money controversy was the final proof that democracy within the states had run amuck. The farm rebellion led by Daniel Shays in Massachusetts in the fall of 1786, and the difficulties the state had in suppressing it, simply confirmed the need for the traditional governing class to reassert its prerogatives.

It is true that by the late 1780s, there was broad public support for strengthening the powers of the Confederation Congress, particularly with regard to matters of interstate and international trade. The delegates who gathered in Philadelphia in 1787, however, had a far more ambitious agenda. The delegates were convinced that what they saw as the excesses of democracy within the states could only be restrained by a radical shift of the power to the federal level and by creating barriers to shield the federal government from what they considered the whims of public opinion. Of the delegates, Alexander Hamilton was the boldest in his proposals. Hamilton suggested that both the President and the members of the Senate should be appointed for life and that the President should have the power to appoint the governor of each state. The other delegates, however, rejected Hamilton's proposal, which was so obviously at odds with the principles of democratic self-government that it would never have been accepted by the people of the thirteen states. Instead, the delegates crafted a document that contained certain democratic features but then placed such severe limits on those features as to render them largely meaningless. One chamber of the proposed Congress, the House of Representatives, was to be directly elected by the voters of each state. The total number of House members, though, was kept small, resulting in large electoral districts in which it would be difficult to secure election in the absence of wealth and prominent name recognition. The interests of southern slave owners were protected by a provision that considered those held in bondage (who, of course, could not vote) as three-fifths of a person for purposes of determining the number of seats each state would receive in the House of Representatives. In addition, any legislation passed by the House of Representatives would only become law if it also received the approval of the Senate and

---

4   Ibid. 140.

the Presidency, neither of which were directly elected by voters. (Congress could overrule a presidential veto by a two-thirds vote of both the House and Senate.) Finally, the judges who apply the law to specific cases would serve for life, and would be appointed by the President, with the approval of the Senate, neither directly elected by voters.

The proposed constitution also contained a long list of specific powers that were stripped from the states. Most notably, states were barred from issuing money (a power reserved exclusively to the newly strengthened federal government), from making any-thing but silver or gold a legal payment for the settling of debts, or from enacting laws that would impair the obligation of contracts. States were thus stripped of very powers that ordinary farmers had made use of to relieve the burden of their excessive debts. Noticeably absent from the proposed federal constitution was a bill of rights along the lines of those contained in most of the state constitutions.

Over the years, some of the Constitution's most anti-democratic features have been modified or scrapped entirely. A massive public outcry, led by anti-Federalist leaders, forced the advocates of the Constitution to agree to the addition of a bill of rights. Slavery was abolished by 13th Amendment to the Constitution, ratified in 1865; and direct election of US Senators was established in 1912, with the ratification of the 17th Amendment. The changes and improvements that have been made to the Constitution over the genera-tions should not, however, blind us to the fundamentally undemocratic structure of the nation's founding political document, an undemocratic structure that remains largely in place to this day.

POSITION #3—A REPUBLIC
OF PROPERTIED MEN
The Constitution in Historical Context

To modern ears, the meaning of the words of the Declaration of Independence is self-evident: "All men are created equal," wrote Thomas Jefferson. "They are endowed by their Creator with certain unalienable Rights, that among these are Life, Liberty and the pursuit of Happiness.—That to secure these rights, Governments are instituted among Men, deriving their just powers from the consent of the governed." What clearer articulation of the modern notion of democratic self-government and equality before the law could there be, particularly if we interpret the term "men" as an anachronistic (and admittedly sexist) term for all humanity? The debate over the US Constitution is often framed as a matter of the degree to which the nation's founding document lived up to the lofty ambitions of the Declaration. Scholars such as Edmund Morgan and Martin Diamond emphasize the Constitution's democratic features and find it a worthy, though imperfect, expression of the principles of the American Revolution. Those such as Charles Beard and Michael Parenti, by contrast, point to the Constitution's elitist elements and find it a betrayal of the democratic vision for which the revolutionaries fought.

To truly understand both the Declaration of Independence and the US Constitution in the context of their times, though, we must set aside our modern assumptions about the nature of politics and government and instead read both documents through the eyes of eighteenth-century American culture. In our modern culture, we assume that it is the individual that is the fundamental building block of society. It is the individual who, through the mechanism of the ballot box, must provide the consent required for government to be legitimate. And it is individuals whose fundamental rights must be respected for the principle of human equality to have meaning. At the time of the American Revolution, however, it was the *household*, rather than the individual, that was assumed to be society's fundamental building block. One's rights and responsibilities were defined by one's place in the household and not by one's status as an individual human being. The eighteenth-century worldview was thus a fundamentally inegalitarian one in which society was assumed to be composed not of free and equal individuals, but of husbands and wives, parents and offspring, and masters and servants all of whose rights and responsibilities were tied to their relationship to a household led by a free, independent, and property-owning head. Looked at this way, the gender, race, and class inequalities built into the constitutional structure of the new nation were not simply flaws within an otherwise democratic republic. Rather, these inequalities were a fundamental and defining component of a republic that was conceived of as a community of free and equal propertied heads of households. The subordination of women, slaves, and others was thus the unequal foundation on which the equality of propertied white men was constructed.

The British colonies in North America were settled for a variety of reasons and took diverse paths of development. The Virginia colony, for instance, began as an entrepreneurial business venture and over time developed a slave-based plantation economy. Massachusetts, by contrast, was founded by a religious sect knows as the Puritans who sought to escape what they considered to be the corruption of England and establish a new society that would operate strictly according to their own interpretation of Christian principles. Massachusetts and the other New England colonies developed as series of tight-knit farming communities that lacked the vast economic inequalities of the slave-based colonies like Virginia. One common characteristic of all of the colonies, however, was the centrality of the household (an institution carried over from England) to the overall social structure. The colonial household was far more than just the location for family life. It was the basic unit of economic production—the place where goods and services were produced. It was where children were raised, and educated, and learned the tools of economic survival. It was a center for daily religious life, as well as the place where the sick, the infirm, and the elderly would be cared for and supported. The household was, in the words of historian John Demos, "a little commonwealth" believed to mirror in microcosm the social relations of the broader social order.[1]

The colonial household was comprised of a set of fixed social positions, each of which had clearly defined roles and responsibilities, as well as a well-understood set of relationships to others in the household. Ultimate authority rested with head of household (also known as the husband). The head was also responsible for representing the household in its dealings with the outside world, with regard to both commercial and civic affairs. The authority of the head, though, was not absolute, as he had certain obligations under the law to the other members of the household. The husband, for instance, could not sell or mortgage the household's real estate without the consent of his wife. The wife was a junior partner in the management of the household with responsibility for the production of a wide range of goods (such as clothing, soap, candles, food storage and preparation) required for daily life. At a relatively young age, a child would became a sort of adult-in-training, providing labor to the household while learning the skills necessary for economic survival under the tutelage of the husband (in the case of sons) or the wife (in the case of daughters). Some households also included servants, a term that referred to any individual who provided labor (be it in the fields, an artisan shop, or in the house and garden) in exchange for legally specified benefits that might include room and board, a cash wage, or (in the case of apprentices) training into a skilled craft. One unique feature of the colonial American household was the presence of slavery. When the first slaves arrived in colonial Virginia, they were originally incorporated into the household structure as servants with the only legal distinction being that a slave's term of service was

---

1   John Demos, *A Little Commonwealth: Family Life in Plymouth Colony* (New York: Oxford University Press, 1970).

perpetual. Over time, slaves were gradually stripped of the legal rights of servants so that ultimately the power of the master over the slave was made absolute in a way that had never been true of other servants.[2]

To sustain a household, a husband had to own sufficient property (or have an artisan skill) to make the household economically viable. Sons and daughters typically remained within the parents' household until they were able to establish, via marriage, an economically viable household of their own. Those men and women unable to establish economically viable households ran the risk of living as perpetual servants in someone else's household. One important difference from England (where property ownership was highly concentrated), was that in colonial America, there was sufficient access to land that the majority of men and women (with the exception of slaves, who were forced into perpetual servitude) could aspire to establish economically viable households.

The meaning of concepts like freedom, equality, and democratic self-rule to Americans of the revolutionary generation must be understood in the context of this household structure. When Jefferson, for instance, wrote of government by consent of the governed, it was taken for granted that it would be the heads of the households who would provide that consent. After all, it was the responsibility of the head to represent the household in its dealings with the broader community. The vote was thus to be restricted to the property-owning males who comprised the household heads of the new nation. Similarly, the unalienable rights to life, liberty, and the pursuit of happiness did not imply equal treatment under the law for all citizens. It went without saying that one's rights were defined by one's position within the household. The legal rights of women, for instance, differed from those of men—and those rights varied depending on a woman's marital status. While married women were generally barred from owning property or entering into contracts in their own name, the unmarried were free to do both. When Jefferson spoke of equality, what he imagined was a nation in which men and women could aspire to establish economically viable households of their own and thus stand as equals in their relations with members of other households, even as the internal structure of the household reproduced inequalities between men and women, between young and old, and between propertied and unpropertied. Slaves, by definition, were to be excluded from this community of free and equal householders as they were, by law, to be kept in perpetual servitude.

None of this, of course, was made explicit in the United States Constitution, as it was so obvious as to not require elaboration. The Constitution was utterly silent, for instance, on the issue of who could or could not vote, leaving that matter to the individual states. State laws, though, reflected the assumption that it was the head that was to represent the household in the affairs of government. At the time of the Revolution, every state had property restrictions on voting. A few states removed these restrictions either during or shortly after the Revolution, but most kept them in place well into the nineteenth century. Every state except New Jersey (which allowed the small number of property-owning women to cast ballots) restricted the vote to men. Issues of slavery and race are more complex. As with

---

2   Edmund S. Morgan, *American Slavery, American Freedom: The Ordeal of Colonial Virginia* (New York: W.W. Norton, 1975), 295–337.

voting rights, the legality of slavery was a matter to be left up to the individual states. At the time of the Revolution, slavery was legal in all thirteen states; though by 1804, each of the northern states had taken steps to abolish it. The words "slavery" and "slave" appear nowhere in the Constitution, but the document did contain a number of provisions designed to buttress the institution, including a requirement that persons "held in Service or Labor in one State" (viz., slaves and indentured servants) who escaped to another state be returned to the masters from whom they had escaped. At the time of the Revolution, only Virginia explicitly barred black men from voting, though a number of states added such a restriction in the years that followed. The notion that slaves should be eligible to vote was, of course, unthinkable; and those held in bondage were barred from the ballot box by property restrictions. (Between the American Revolution and the Civil War, explicit racial restrictions on voting spread to the majority of states, both North and South. The New England states resisted this trend.)

The United States Constitution was written by a group of men who assumed that democratic self-rule entailed independent propertied heads of household coming together to govern the affairs of the community and of the nation. As historian Jan Lewis explains, women were to be represented but were not permitted to represent themselves.[3] The same could be said for the other subordinated members of the household. Nowhere in the Constitution were women, slaves, and the unpropertied explicitly excluded from the rights and responsibilities of equal democratic citizenship. In a world in which daily life was shaped by one's place within a strictly defined household structure, however, this silence represented a tacit embrace of the inequalities inherent in the colonial American household.

---

3   Jan Lewis, "Of Every Sex & Condition: The Representation of Women in the Constitution," *Journal of the Early Republic* 15(Autumn 1995), 369.

DEBATING THE QUESTION

DECLARATIONS AND CONSTITUTIONS

In the Declaration of Independence of 1776, the leaders of American Revolution proclaimed equality, liberty, and right to self-government to be the foundation upon which their new nation would be constructed. The Constitution of 1787 established a specific set of rules by which the government of the newly independent United States would operate. To what degree did those rules actually allow the people of the country to govern themselves on the basis of equality? Answering that question requires a careful review of the US Constitution and the rules that it established. It may also be useful to contrast the system of government established by the Constitution with that in operation under the Articles of Confederation and constitutions of the various states. How democratic, for instance, was the new federal constitution when compared to the constitutions of states like Virginia and Pennsylvania?

1.1 THE DECLARATION OF INDEPENDENCE (1776)

The debate among historians over the US Constitution is often framed as a matter of the degree to which the nation's founding document lived up to the democratic tendencies unleashed by the American Revolution. For that reason, it may be useful to look at Declaration of Independence to see what revolutionary leaders said they were fighting for. Keep in mind that the Declaration was, more than anything else, an argument for independence from Britain. From the perspective of the British, the revolutionaries were engaged in an act of treason. The revolutionaries had to make the case, both to residents of the colonies and to foreign powers, that they were justified in taking up arms and for declaring independence. In making this case, Thomas Jefferson (the primary author of the Declaration) offered a set of principles on which legitimate government power should rest.

GUIDING QUESTIONS:

1. Where in the Declaration of Independence does Jefferson most clearly present his theory of government?
2. From where does Jefferson say governments derive their legitimate powers?

THE DECLARATION OF INDEPENDENCE (1776)

IN CONGRESS, July 4, 1776.

THE UNANIMOUS DECLARATION OF THE THIRTEEN UNITED STATES OF AMERICA,

When in the Course of human events, it becomes necessary for one people to dissolve the political bands which have connected them with another, and to assume among the powers of the earth, the separate and equal station to which the Laws of Nature and of Nature's God entitle them, a decent respect to the opinions of mankind requires that they should declare the causes which impel them to the separation.

We hold these truths to be self-evident, that all men are created equal, that they are endowed by their Creator with certain unalienable Rights, that among these are Life, Liberty and the pursuit of Happiness.—That to secure these rights, Governments are instituted among Men, deriving their just powers from the consent of the governed,—That whenever any Form of Government becomes destructive of these ends, it is the Right of the People to alter or to abolish it, and to institute new Government, laying its foundation on such principles and organizing its powers in such form, as to them shall seem most likely to effect their Safety and Happiness. Prudence, indeed, will dictate that Governments long established should not be changed for light and transient causes; and accordingly all experience hath shewn, that mankind are more disposed to suffer, while evils are sufferable, than to right themselves by abolishing the forms to which they are accustomed. But when a long train of abuses and usurpations, pursuing invariably the same Object evinces a design to reduce them under absolute Despotism, it is their right, it is their duty, to throw off such Government, and to provide new Guards for their future security.—Such has been the patient sufferance of these Colonies; and such is now the

Declaration of Independence: A Transcription, National Archives and Records Administration, https://www.archives.gov/founding-docs/declaration-transcript

necessity which constrains them to alter their former Systems of Government. The history of the present King of Great Britain is a history of repeated injuries and usurpations, all having in direct object the establishment of an absolute Tyranny over these States. To prove this, let Facts be submitted to a candid world.

He has refused his Assent to Laws, the most wholesome and necessary for the public good.

He has forbidden his Governors to pass Laws of immediate and pressing importance, unless suspended in their operation till his Assent should be obtained; and when so suspended, he has utterly neglected to attend to them.

He has refused to pass other Laws for the accommodation of large districts of people, unless those people would relinquish the right of Representation in the Legislature, a right inestimable to them and formidable to tyrants only.

He has called together legislative bodies at places unusual, uncomfortable, and distant from the depository of their public Records, for the sole purpose of fatiguing them into compliance with his measures.

He has dissolved Representative Houses repeatedly, for opposing with manly firmness his invasions on the rights of the people.

He has refused for a long time, after such dissolutions, to cause others to be elected; whereby the Legislative powers, incapable of Annihilation, have returned to the People at large for their exercise; the State remaining in the mean time exposed to all the dangers of invasion from without, and convulsions within.

He has endeavoured to prevent the population of these States; for that purpose obstructing the Laws for Naturalization of Foreigners; refusing to pass others to encourage their migrations hither, and raising the conditions of new Appropriations of Lands.

He has obstructed the Administration of Justice, by refusing his Assent to Laws for establishing Judiciary powers.

He has made Judges dependent on his Will alone, for the tenure of their offices, and the amount and payment of their salaries.

He has erected a multitude of New Offices, and sent hither swarms of Officers to harrass our people, and eat out their substance.

He has kept among us, in times of peace, Standing Armies without the Consent of our legislatures.

He has affected to render the Military independent of and superior to the Civil power.

He has combined with others to subject us to a jurisdiction foreign to our constitution, and unacknowledged by our laws; giving his Assent to their Acts of pretended Legislation:

For Quartering large bodies of armed troops among us:

For protecting them, by a mock Trial, from punishment for any Murders which they should commit on the Inhabitants of these States:

For cutting off our Trade with all parts of the world:

For imposing Taxes on us without our Consent:

For depriving us in many cases, of the benefits of Trial by Jury:

For transporting us beyond Seas to be tried for pretended offences

For abolishing the free System of English Laws in a neighbouring Province, establishing therein an Arbitrary government, and enlarging its Boundaries so as to render it at once an example and fit instrument for introducing the same absolute rule into these Colonies:

For taking away our Charters, abolishing our most valuable Laws, and altering fundamentally the Forms of our Governments:

For suspending our own Legislatures, and declaring themselves invested with power to legislate for us in all cases whatsoever.

He has abdicated Government here, by declaring us out of his Protection and waging War against us.

He has plundered our seas, ravaged our Coasts, burnt our towns, and destroyed the lives of our people.

He is at this time transporting large Armies of foreign Mercenaries to compleat the works of death, desolation and tyranny, already begun with circumstances of Cruelty & perfidy scarcely paralleled in the most barbarous ages, and totally unworthy the Head of a civilized nation.

He has constrained our fellow Citizens taken Captive on the high Seas to bear Arms against their

Country, to become the executioners of their friends and Brethren, or to fall themselves by their Hands.

He has excited domestic insurrections amongst us, and has endeavoured to bring on the inhabitants of our frontiers, the merciless Indian Savages, whose known rule of warfare, is an undistinguished destruction of all ages, sexes and conditions.

In every stage of these Oppressions We have Petitioned for Redress in the most humble terms: Our repeated Petitions have been answered only by repeated injury. A Prince whose character is thus marked by every act which may define a Tyrant, is unfit to be the ruler of a free people.

Nor have We been wanting in attentions to our Brittish brethren. We have warned them from time to time of attempts by their legislature to extend an unwarrantable jurisdiction over us. We have reminded them of the circumstances of our emigration and settlement here. We have appealed to their native justice and magnanimity, and we have conjured them by the ties of our common kindred to disavow these usurpations, which, would inevitably interrupt our connections and correspondence. They too have been deaf to the voice of justice and of consanguinity. We must, therefore, acquiesce in the necessity, which denounces our Separation, and hold them, as we hold the rest of mankind, Enemies in War, in Peace Friends.

We, therefore, the Representatives of the united States of America, in General Congress, Assembled, appealing to the Supreme Judge of the world for the rectitude of our intentions, do, in the Name, and by Authority of the good People of these Colonies, solemnly publish and declare, That these United Colonies are, and of Right ought to be Free and Independent States; that they are Absolved from all Allegiance to the British Crown, and that all political connection between them and the State of Great Britain, is and ought to be totally dissolved; and that as Free and Independent States, they have full Power to levy War, conclude Peace, contract Alliances, establish Commerce, and to do all other Acts and Things which Independent States may of right do. And for the support of this Declaration, with a firm reliance on the protection of divine Providence, we mutually pledge to each other our Lives, our Fortunes and our sacred Honor.

DRAWING CONCLUSION:

1. How democratic is the theory of government presented in the Declaration of Independence? (A democratic theory of government is one that emphasizes both the right and the ability of a group of people to govern themselves.)

1.2 THE ARTICLES OF CONFEDERATION (1777)

To evaluate the motives of the Federalists and the constitution they created, it is helpful to examine the Articles of Confederation, the document that they sought to replace. The Articles of Confederation declared the United States of America to be a "firm league of friendship" among sovereign states. It established a federal Congress and granted that body certain important but limited powers. It also established methods for the selection of representatives to Congress and rules for how Congress would make decisions. Finally, it placed certain limits on the authority of the individual states. As you read the Articles of Confederation, your most important task will be to identify the most important rules and procedures it established for the operation of the federal government as well as for the individual states.

GUIDING QUESTIONS:

1. Identify the specific place in the Articles of Confederation where each of the following can be found:
    a. The method for choosing representatives to Congress.
    b. The distribution of votes in Congress among the states.
    c. The specific powers of the Congress.
    d. The decision-making process in Congress (ie., the number of votes required to make various types of decisions.)
    e. The powers of the state governments
    f. The limits on the powers of the state governments.
2. What are the actual provisions in the Articles of Confederation for each of the preceding items?

THE ARTICLES OF CONFEDERATION

To all to whom these Presents shall come, we the undersigned Delegates of the States affixed to our Names send greeting.

Articles of Confederation and perpetual Union between the states of New Hampshire, Massachusetts-bay Rhode Island and Providence Plantations, Connecticut, New York, New Jersey, Pennsylvania, Delaware, Maryland, Virginia, North Carolina, South Carolina and Georgia.

I.

The Stile of this Confederacy shall be "The United States of America."

II.

Each state retains its sovereignty, freedom, and independence, and every power, jurisdiction, and right, which is not by this Confederation expressly delegated to the United States, in Congress assembled.

Articles of Confederation and Perpetual Union Between the States (Williamsburg: Alexander Purdie, 1777), online facsimile at https://www.loc.gov/item/rbpe.17802600/

III.

The said States hereby severally enter into a firm league of friendship with each other, for their common defense, the security of their liberties, and their mutual and general welfare, binding themselves to assist each other, against all force offered to, or attacks made upon them, or any of them, on account of religion, sovereignty, trade, or any other pretense whatever.

IV.

The better to secure and perpetuate mutual friendship and intercourse among the people of the different States in this Union, the free inhabitants of each of these States, paupers, vagabonds, and fugitives from justice excepted, shall be entitled to all privileges and immunities of free citizens in the several States; and the people of each State shall free ingress and regress to and from any other State, and shall enjoy therein all the privileges of trade and commerce, subject to the same duties, impositions, and restrictions as the inhabitants thereof respectively, provided that such restrictions shall not extend so far as to prevent the removal of property imported into any State, to any other State, of which the owner is an inhabitant; provided also that no imposition, duties or restriction shall be laid by any State, on the property of the United States, or either of them.

If any person guilty of, or charged with, treason, felony, or other high misdemeanor in any State, shall flee from justice, and be found in any of the United States, he shall, upon demand of the Governor or executive power of the State from which he fled, be delivered up and removed to the State having jurisdiction of his offense.

Full faith and credit shall be given in each of these States to the records, acts, and judicial proceedings of the courts and magistrats of every other State.

V.

For the most convenient management of the general interests of the United States, delegates shall be annually appointed in such manner as the legislatures of each State shall direct, to meet in Congress on the first Monday in November, in every year, with a power reserved to each State to recall its delegates, or any of them, at any time within the year, and to send others in their stead for the remainder of the year.

No State shall be represented in Congress by less than two, nor more than seven members; and no person shall be capable of being a delegate for more than three years in any term of six years; nor shall any person, being a delegate, be capable of holding any office under the United States, for which he, or another for his benefit, receives any salary, fees or emolument of any kind.

Each State shall maintain its own delegates in a meeting of the States, and while they act as members of the committee of the States.

In determining questions in the United States in Congress assembled, each State shall have one vote.

Freedom of speech and debate in Congress shall not be impeached or questioned in any court or place out of Congress, and the members of Congress shall be protected in their persons from arrests or imprisonments, during the time of their going to and from, and attendence on Congress, except for treason, felony, or breach of the peace.

VI.

No State, without the consent of the United States in Congress assembled, shall send any embassy to, or receive any embassy from, or enter into any conference, agreement, alliance or treaty with any King, Prince or State; nor shall any person holding any office of profit or trust under the United States, or any of them, accept any present, emolument, office or title of any kind whatever from any King, Prince or foreign State; nor shall the United States in Congress assembled, or any of them, grant any title of nobility.

No two or more States shall enter into any treaty, confederation or alliance whatever between them, without the consent of the United States in Congress assembled, specifying accurately the purposes for which the same is to be entered into, and how long it shall continue.

No State shall lay any imposts or duties, which may interfere with any stipulations in treaties, entered into by the United States in Congress assembled, with any King, Prince or State, in pursuance of any treaties already proposed by Congress, to the courts of France and Spain.

No vessel of war shall be kept up in time of peace by any State, except such number only, as shall be deemed necessary by the United States in Congress assembled, for the defense of such State, or its trade; nor shall any body of forces be kept up by any State in time of peace, except such number only, as in the judgement of the United States in Congress assembled, shall be deemed requisite to garrison the forts necessary for the defense of such State; but every State shall always keep up a well-regulated and disciplined militia, sufficiently armed and accoutered, and shall provide and constantly have ready for use, in public stores, a due number of filed pieces and tents, and a proper quantity of arms, ammunition and camp equipage.

No State shall engage in any war without the consent of the United States in Congress assembled, unless such State be actually invaded by enemies, or shall have received certain advice of a resolution being formed by some nation of Indians to invade such State, and the danger is so imminent as not to admit of a delay till the United States in Congress assembled can be consulted; nor shall any State grant commissions to any ships or vessels of war, nor letters of marque or reprisal, except it be after a declaration of war by the United States in Congress assembled, and then only against the Kingdom or State and the subjects thereof, against which war has been so declared, and under such regulations as shall be established by the United States in Congress assembled, unless such State be infested by pirates, in which case vessels of war may be fitted out for that occasion, and kept so long as the danger shall continue, or until the United States in Congress assembled shall determine otherwise.

VII.

When land forces are raised by any State for the common defense, all officers of or under the rank of colonel, shall be appointed by the legislature of each State respectively, by whom such forces shall be raised, or in such manner as such State shall direct, and all vacancies shall be filled up by the State which first made the appointment.

VIII.

All charges of war, and all other expenses that shall be incurred for the common defense or general welfare, and allowed by the United States in Congress assembled, shall be defrayed out of a common treasury, which shall be supplied by the several States in proportion to the value of all land within each State, granted or surveyed for any person, as such land and the buildings and improvements thereon shall be estimated according to such mode as the United States in Congress assembled, shall from time to time direct and appoint.

The taxes for paying that proportion shall be laid and levied by the authority and direction of the legislatures of the several States within the time agreed upon by the United States in Congress assembled.

IX.

The United States in Congress assembled, shall have the sole and exclusive right and power of determining on peace and war, except in the cases mentioned in the sixth article

- of sending and receiving ambassadors
- entering into treaties and alliances, provided that no treaty of commerce shall be made whereby the legislative power of the respective States shall be restrained from imposing such imposts and duties on foreigners, as their own people are subjected to, or from prohibiting the exportation or importation of any species of goods or commodities whatsoever
- of establishing rules for deciding in all cases, what captures on land or water shall be legal, and in what manner prizes taken by land or naval forces in the service of the United States shall be divided or appropriated
- of granting letters of marque and reprisal in times of peace
- appointing courts for the trial of piracies and felonies commited on the high seas and establishing courts for receiving and determining finally appeals in all cases of captures, provided that no member of Congress shall be appointed a judge of any of the said courts.

The United States in Congress assembled shall also be the last resort on appeal in all disputes and differences now subsisting or that hereafter may arise between two or more States concerning boundary, jurisdiction or any other causes whatever; which authority shall always be exercised in the manner following.

Whenever the legislative or executive authority or lawful agent of any State in controversy with another shall present a petition to Congress stating the matter in question and praying for a hearing, notice thereof shall be given by order of Congress to the legislative or executive authority of the other State in controversy, and a day assigned for the appearance of the parties by their lawful agents, who shall then be directed to appoint by joint consent, commissioners or judges to constitute a court for hearing and determining the matter in question: but if they cannot agree, Congress shall name three persons out of each of the United States, and from the list of such persons each party shall alternately strike out one, the petitioners beginning, until the number shall be reduced to thirteen; and from that number not less than seven, nor more than nine names as Congress shall direct, shall in the presence of Congress be drawn out by lot, and the persons whose names shall be so drawn or any five of them, shall be commissioners or judges, to hear and finally determine the controversy, so always as a major part of the judges who shall hear the cause shall agree in the determination: and if either party shall neglect to attend at the day appointed, without showing reasons, which Congress shall judge sufficient, or being present shall refuse to strike, the Congress shall proceed to nominate three persons out of each State, and the secretary of Congress shall strike in behalf of such party absent or refusing; and the judgement and sentence of the court to be appointed, in the manner before prescribed, shall be final and conclusive; and if any of the parties shall refuse to submit to the authority of such court, or to appear or defend their claim or cause, the court shall nevertheless proceed to pronounce sentence, or judgement, which shall in like manner be final and decisive, the judgement or sentence and other proceedings being in either case transmitted to Congress, and lodged among the acts of Congress for the security of the parties concerned: provided that every commissioner, before he sits in judgement, shall take an oath to be administered by one of the judges of the supreme or superior court of the State, where the cause shall be tried, 'well and truly to hear and determine the matter in question, according to the best of his judgement, without favor, affection or hope of reward': provided also, that no State shall be deprived of territory for the benefit of the United States.

All controversies concerning the private right of soil claimed under different grants of two or more States, whose jurisdictions as they may respect such lands, and the States which passed such grants are adjusted, the said grants or either of them being at the same time claimed to have originated antecedent to such settlement of jurisdiction, shall on the petition of either party to the Congress of the United States, be finally determined as near as may be in the same manner as is before prescribed for deciding disputes respecting territorial jurisdiction between different States.

The United States in Congress assembled shall also have the sole and exclusive right and power of regulating the alloy and value of coin struck by their own authority, or by that of the respective States

- fixing the standards of weights and measures throughout the United States
- regulating the trade and managing all affairs with the Indians, not members of any of the States, provided that the legislative right of any State within its own limits be not infringed or violated
- establishing or regulating post offices from one State to another, throughout all the United States, and exacting such postage on the papers passing through the same as may be requisite to defray the expenses of the said office
- appointing all officers of the land forces, in the service of the United States, excepting regimental officers
- appointing all the officers of the naval forces, and commissioning all officers whatever in the service of the United States
- making rules for the government and regulation of the said land and naval forces, and directing their operations.

The United States in Congress assembled shall have authority to appoint a committee, to sit in the recess of Congress, to be denominated 'A Committee of the States', and to consist of one delegate from each State; and to appoint such other committees and civil officers as may be necessary for managing the general affairs of the United States under their direction

- to appoint one of their members to preside, provided that no person be allowed to serve in the office of president more than one year in any term of three years; to ascertain the necessary sums of money to be raised for the service of the United States, and to appropriate and apply the same for defraying the public expenses

- to borrow money, or emit bills on the credit of the United States, transmitting every half-year to the respective States an account of the sums of money so borrowed or emitted
- to build and equip a navy
- to agree upon the number of land forces, and to make requisitions from each State for its quota, in proportion to the number of white inhabitants in such State; which requisition shall be binding, and thereupon the legislature of each State shall appoint the regimental officers, raise the men and cloath, arm and equip them in a solid-like manner, at the expense of the United States; and the officers and men so cloathed, armed and equipped shall march to the place appointed, and within the time agreed on by the United States in Congress assembled. But if the United States in Congress assembled shall, on consideration of circumstances judge proper that any State should not raise men, or should raise a smaller number of men than the quota thereof, such extra number shall be raised, officered, cloathed, armed and equipped in the same manner as the quota of each State, unless the legislature of such State shall judge that such extra number cannot be safely spread out in the same, in which case they shall raise, officer, cloath, arm and equip as many of such extra number as they judge can be safely spared. And the officers and men so cloathed, armed, and equipped, shall march to the place appointed, and within the time agreed on by the United States in Congress assembled.

The United States in Congress assembled shall never engage in a war, nor grant letters of marque or reprisal in time of peace, nor enter into any treaties or alliances, nor coin money, nor regulate the value thereof, nor ascertain the sums and expenses necessary for the defense and welfare of the United States, or any of them, nor emit bills, nor borrow money on the credit of the United States, nor appropriate money, nor agree upon the number of vessels of war, to be built or purchased, or the number of land or sea forces to be raised, nor appoint a commander in chief of the army or navy, unless nine States assent to the same: nor shall a question on any other point, except for adjourning from day to day be determined, unless by the votes of the majority of the United States in Congress assembled.

The Congress of the United States shall have power to adjourn to any time within the year, and to any place within the United States, so that no period of adjournment be for a longer duration than the space of six months, and shall publish the journal of their proceedings monthly, except such parts thereof relating to treaties, alliances or military operations, as in their judgement require secrecy; and the yeas and nays of the delegates of each State on any question shall be entered on the journal, when it is desired by any delegates of a State, or any of them, at his or their request shall be furnished with a transcript of the said journal, except such parts as are above excepted, to lay before the legislatures of the several States.

X.

The Committee of the States, or any nine of them, shall be authorized to execute, in the recess of Congress, such of the powers of Congress as the United States in Congress assembled, by the consent of the nine States, shall from time to time think expedient to vest them with; provided that no power be delegated to the said Committee, for the exercise of which, by the Articles of Confederation, the voice of nine States in the Congress of the United States assembled be requisite.

XI.

Canada acceding to this confederation, and adjoining in the measures of the United States, shall be admitted into, and entitled to all the advantages of this Union; but no other colony shall be admitted into the same, unless such admission be agreed to by nine States.

XII.

All bills of credit emitted, monies borrowed, and debts contracted by, or under the authority of Congress, before the assembling of the United States, in pursuance of the present confederation, shall be deemed and considered as a charge against the

United States, for payment and satisfaction whereof the said United States, and the public faith are hereby solemnly pleged.

XIII.

Every State shall abide by the determination of the United States in Congress assembled, on all questions which by this confederation are submitted to them. And the Articles of this Confederation shall be inviolably observed by every State, and the Union shall be perpetual; nor shall any alteration at any time hereafter be made in any of them; unless such alteration be agreed to in a Congress of the United States, and be afterwards confirmed by the legislatures of every State.

And Whereas it hath pleased the Great Governor of the World to incline the hearts of the legislatures we respectively represent in Congress, to approve of, and to authorize us to ratify the said Articles of Confederation and perpetual Union. Know Ye that we the undersigned delegates, by virtue of the power and authority to us given for that purpose, do by these presents, in the name and in behalf of our respective constituents, fully and entirely ratify and confirm each and every of the said Articles of Confederation and perpetual Union, and all and singular the matters and things therein contained: And we do further solemnly plight and engage the faith of our respective constituents, that they shall abide by the determinations of the United States in Congress assembled, on all questions, which by the said Confederation are submitted to them. And that the Articles thereof shall be inviolably observed by the States we respectively represent, and that the Union shall be perpetual.

In Witness whereof we have hereunto set our hands in Congress. Done at Philadelphia in the State of Pennsylvania the ninth day of July in the Year of our Lord One Thousand Seven Hundred and Seventy-Eight, and in the Third Year of the independence of America.

DRAWING CONCLUSIONS:

1. Explain, in your own words, the key provisions of the Articles of Confederation regarding
   a. The method for choosing representatives to Congress.
   b. The distribution of votes in Congress among the states.
   c. The specific powers of the Congress.
   d. The decision-making process in Congress (i.e., the number of votes required to make various types of decisions).
   e. The powers of the state governments.
   f. The limits on the powers of the state governments.

1.3 THE CONSTITUTION OF THE UNITED STATES (1787)

To determine how democratic the Constitution of the United States was, the most important evidence is, of course, the Constitution itself. The Constitution, however, can be difficult to read and understand. It is a complex document (far more complex than the Articles), and it is written in technical legal language. It is helpful, though, to think of the Constitution as simply establishing a set of rules by which the government would operate. In working with the Constitution, your main task will be first to identify and understand the key rules and then to judge how democratic these rules actually were. To what extent did these rules allow the people of the United States to govern themselves (especially when contrasted with the Articles of Confederation)?

It is also helpful to have a framework for understanding the Constitution. The Constitution established a set of rules that did the following things:

1. Put in place three branches of government: (a) a legislative branch (called the Congress) whose main function was to enact laws (the Congress contained two houses called the House of Representatives and the Senate); (b) an executive branch headed by a President whose main function was to conduct the day-to-day operations of the government; (c) a judicial branch made up of federal courts (including a Supreme Court) whose main function was to determine how the laws enacted by Congress should be applied in specific cases.
2. Establish procedures for selecting the Congress, the President, and federal judges.
3. Delegate specific powers to each of the branches of the federal government.
4. Place limits on the powers of the federal government.
5. Place limits on the powers of the state governments.

As you will see, the powers granted to the federal government were far more extensive than under the Articles of Confederation as were the limits on powers of the state governments.

The Constitution was divided up into seven articles. To help you navigate the document, here is a summary of the contents of each article:

- Article I—The Congress/Legislative Branch
- Article II—The President/Executive Branch
- Article III—The Federal Courts/Judicial Branch
- Article IV—The rights and responsibilities of the states to each other/the relationship between the states and the federal government
- Article V—Procedures for amending the Constitution
- Article VI—Provisions that did not easily fit other Articles
- Article VII—Provisions for initial ratification of the Constitution

Be careful, though—some provisions are not where you might expect them. The procedures for selecting federal judges, for instance, are not found in Article III.

GUIDING QUESTIONS:

1. Identify the specific places in the Constitution where the following can be found. Keep in mind that in some cases, the provisions will be found in more than one place.
   a. The methods for choosing the members of each branch _____
      i. The methods for choosing members of the House of Representatives and Senate

ii. The method for choosing the President

iii. The method for choosing federal judges

b. The powers of each branch

  i. The powers of the Congress (note places where the House and Senate share a specific power as well as places where a specific power is given to either the House or Senate)

  ii. The powers of the President

  iii. The powers of the federal courts

c. Limits on the powers of the various branches

d. The decision-making process in Congress (i.e., the number of votes required to make various types of decisions)

e. The limits on the powers of the state governments.

2. What are the actual provisions in the Constitution for each of the preceding items? Focus in on what you consider to be the key provision.

THE CONSTITUTION OF THE UNITED STATES

We the People of the United States, in Order to form a more perfect Union, establish Justice, insure domestic Tranquility, provide for the common defence, promote the general Welfare, and secure the Blessings of Liberty to ourselves and our Posterity, do ordain and establish this Constitution for the United States of America.

ARTICLE I.

Section. 1.

All legislative Powers herein granted shall be vested in a Congress of the United States, which shall consist of a Senate and House of Representatives.

Section. 2.

The House of Representatives shall be composed of Members chosen every second Year by the People of the several States, and the Electors in each State shall have the Qualifications requisite for Electors of the most numerous Branch of the State Legislature.

No Person shall be a Representative who shall not have attained to the Age of twenty five Years, and been seven Years a Citizen of the United States, and who shall not, when elected, be an Inhabitant of that State in which he shall be chosen.

Representatives and direct Taxes shall be apportioned among the several States which may be included within this Union, according to their respective Numbers, which shall be determined by adding to the whole Number of free Persons, including those bound to Service for a Term of Years, and excluding Indians not taxed, three fifths of all other Persons. The actual Enumeration shall be made within three Years after the first Meeting of the Congress of the United States, and within every subsequent Term of ten Years, in such Manner as they shall by Law direct. The Number of Representatives shall not exceed one for every thirty Thousand, but each State shall have at Least one Representative; and until such enumeration shall be made, the State of New Hampshire shall be entitled to chuse three, Massachusetts eight, Rhode-Island and Providence Plantations one, Connecticut five, New-York six, New Jersey four, Pennsylvania eight, Delaware one, Maryland six, Virginia ten, North Carolina five, South Carolina five, and Georgia three.

When vacancies happen in the Representation from any State, the Executive Authority thereof shall issue Writs of Election to fill such Vacancies.

The House of Representatives shall chuse their Speaker and other Officers; and shall have the sole Power of Impeachment.

The Constitution of the United States: A Transcription, National Archives and Records Administration, https://www.archives.gov/founding-docs/constitution-transcript

Section. 3.

The Senate of the United States shall be composed of two Senators from each State, chosen by the Legislature thereof for six Years; and each Senator shall have one Vote.

Immediately after they shall be assembled in Consequence of the first Election, they shall be divided as equally as may be into three Classes. The Seats of the Senators of the first Class shall be vacated at the Expiration of the second Year, of the second Class at the Expiration of the fourth Year, and of the third Class at the Expiration of the sixth Year, so that one third may be chosen every second Year; and if Vacancies happen by Resignation, or otherwise, during the Recess of the Legislature of any State, the Executive thereof may make temporary Appointments until the next Meeting of the Legislature, which shall then fill such Vacancies.

No Person shall be a Senator who shall not have attained to the Age of thirty Years, and been nine Years a Citizen of the United States, and who shall not, when elected, be an Inhabitant of that State for which he shall be chosen.

The Vice President of the United States shall be President of the Senate, but shall have no Vote, unless they be equally divided.

The Senate shall chuse their other Officers, and also a President pro tempore, in the Absence of the Vice President, or when he shall exercise the Office of President of the United States.

The Senate shall have the sole Power to try all Impeachments. When sitting for that Purpose, they shall be on Oath or Affirmation. When the President of the United States is tried, the Chief Justice shall preside: And no Person shall be convicted without the Concurrence of two thirds of the Members present.

Judgment in Cases of Impeachment shall not extend further than to removal from Office, and disqualification to hold and enjoy any Office of honor, Trust or Profit under the United States: but the Party convicted shall nevertheless be liable and subject to Indictment, Trial, Judgment and Punishment, according to Law.

Section. 4.

The Times, Places and Manner of holding Elections for Senators and Representatives, shall be prescribed in each State by the Legislature thereof; but the Congress may at any time by Law make or alter such Regulations, except as to the Places of chusing Senators.

The Congress shall assemble at least once in every Year, and such Meeting shall be on the first Monday in December, unless they shall by Law appoint a different Day.

Section. 5.

Each House shall be the Judge of the Elections, Returns and Qualifications of its own Members, and a Majority of each shall constitute a Quorum to do Business; but a smaller Number may adjourn from day to day, and may be authorized to compel the Attendance of absent Members, in such Manner, and under such Penalties as each House may provide.

Each House may determine the Rules of its Proceedings, punish its Members for disorderly Behaviour, and, with the Concurrence of two thirds, expel a Member.

Each House shall keep a Journal of its Proceedings, and from time to time publish the same, excepting such Parts as may in their Judgment require Secrecy; and the Yeas and Nays of the Members of either House on any question shall, at the Desire of one fifth of those Present, be entered on the Journal.

Neither House, during the Session of Congress, shall, without the Consent of the other, adjourn for more than three days, nor to any other Place than that in which the two Houses shall be sitting.

Section. 6.

The Senators and Representatives shall receive a Compensation for their Services, to be ascertained by Law, and paid out of the Treasury of the United States. They shall in all Cases, except Treason, Felony and Breach of the Peace, be privileged from Arrest during their Attendance at the Session of their respective Houses, and in going to and returning from the same; and for any Speech or Debate in either House, they shall not be questioned in any other Place.

No Senator or Representative shall, during the Time for which he was elected, be appointed to any civil Office under the Authority of the United States, which shall have been created, or the Emoluments whereof shall have been encreased during such time; and no Person holding any Office under the United States, shall be a Member of either House during his Continuance in Office.

Section. 7.

All Bills for raising Revenue shall originate in the House of Representatives; but the Senate may propose or concur with Amendments as on other Bills.

Every Bill which shall have passed the House of Representatives and the Senate, shall, before it become a Law, be presented to the President of the United States: If he approve he shall sign it, but if not he shall return it, with his Objections to that House in which it shall have originated, who shall enter the Objections at large on their Journal, and proceed to reconsider it. If after such Reconsideration two thirds of that House shall agree to pass the Bill, it shall be sent, together with the Objections, to the other House, by which it shall likewise be reconsidered, and if approved by two thirds of that House, it shall become a Law. But in all such Cases the Votes of both Houses shall be determined by yeas and Nays, and the Names of the Persons voting for and against the Bill shall be entered on the Journal of each House respectively. If any Bill shall not be returned by the President within ten Days (Sundays excepted) after it shall have been presented to him, the Same shall be a Law, in like Manner as if he had signed it, unless the Congress by their Adjournment prevent its Return, in which Case it shall not be a Law.

Every Order, Resolution, or Vote to which the Concurrence of the Senate and House of Representatives may be necessary (except on a question of Adjournment) shall be presented to the President of the United States; and before the Same shall take Effect, shall be approved by him, or being disapproved by him, shall be repassed by two thirds of the Senate and House of Representatives, according to the Rules and Limitations prescribed in the Case of a Bill.

Section. 8.

The Congress shall have Power To lay and collect Taxes, Duties, Imposts and Excises, to pay the Debts and provide for the common Defence and general Welfare of the United States; but all Duties, Imposts and Excises shall be uniform throughout the United States;

To borrow Money on the credit of the United States;

To regulate Commerce with foreign Nations, and among the several States, and with the Indian Tribes;

To establish an uniform Rule of Naturalization, and uniform Laws on the subject of Bankruptcies throughout the United States;

To coin Money, regulate the Value thereof, and of foreign Coin, and fix the Standard of Weights and Measures;

To provide for the Punishment of counterfeiting the Securities and current Coin of the United States;

To establish Post Offices and post Roads;

To promote the Progress of Science and useful Arts, by securing for limited Times to Authors and Inventors the exclusive Right to their respective Writings and Discoveries;

To constitute Tribunals inferior to the supreme Court;

To define and punish Piracies and Felonies committed on the high Seas, and Offences against the Law of Nations;

To declare War, grant Letters of Marque and Reprisal, and make Rules concerning Captures on Land and Water;

To raise and support Armies, but no Appropriation of Money to that Use shall be for a longer Term than two Years;

To provide and maintain a Navy;

To make Rules for the Government and Regulation of the land and naval Forces;

To provide for calling forth the Militia to execute the Laws of the Union, suppress Insurrections and repel Invasions;

To provide for organizing, arming, and disciplining, the Militia, and for governing such Part of them as may be employed in the Service of the United States, reserving to the States respectively, the Appointment of the Officers, and the Authority of training the Militia according to the discipline prescribed by Congress;

To exercise exclusive Legislation in all Cases whatsoever, over such District (not exceeding ten Miles square) as may, by Cession of particular States, and the Acceptance of Congress, become the Seat of the Government of the United States, and to exercise like Authority over all Places purchased by the Consent of the Legislature of the State in which the Same shall be, for the Erection of Forts, Magazines, Arsenals, dockYards, and other needful Buildings;—And

To make all Laws which shall be necessary and proper for carrying into Execution the foregoing Powers, and all other Powers vested by this Constitution in the Government of the United States, or in any Department or Officer thereof.

Section. 9.

The Migration or Importation of such Persons as any of the States now existing shall think proper to admit, shall not be prohibited by the Congress prior to the Year one thousand eight hundred and eight, but a Tax or duty may be imposed on such Importation, not exceeding ten dollars for each Person.

The Privilege of the Writ of Habeas Corpus shall not be suspended, unless when in Cases of Rebellion or Invasion the public Safety may require it.

No Bill of Attainder or ex post facto Law shall be passed.

No Capitation, or other direct, Tax shall be laid, unless in Proportion to the Census or enumeration herein before directed to be taken.

No Tax or Duty shall be laid on Articles exported from any State.

No Preference shall be given by any Regulation of Commerce or Revenue to the Ports of one State over those of another; nor shall Vessels bound to, or from, one State, be obliged to enter, clear, or pay Duties in another.

No Money shall be drawn from the Treasury, but in Consequence of Appropriations made by Law; and a regular Statement and Account of the Receipts and Expenditures of all public Money shall be published from time to time.

No Title of Nobility shall be granted by the United States: And no Person holding any Office of Profit or Trust under them, shall, without the Consent of the Congress, accept of any present, Emolument, Office, or Title, of any kind whatever, from any King, Prince, or foreign State.

Section. 10.

No State shall enter into any Treaty, Alliance, or Confederation; grant Letters of Marque and Reprisal; coin Money; emit Bills of Credit; make any Thing but gold and silver Coin a Tender in Payment of Debts; pass any Bill of Attainder, ex post facto Law, or Law impairing the Obligation of Contracts, or grant any Title of Nobility.

No State shall, without the Consent of the Congress, lay any Imposts or Duties on Imports or Exports, except what may be absolutely necessary for executing it's inspection Laws: and the net Produce of all Duties and Imposts, laid by any State on Imports or Exports, shall be for the Use of the Treasury of the United States; and all such Laws shall be subject to the Revision and Controul of the Congress.

No State shall, without the Consent of Congress, lay any Duty of Tonnage, keep Troops, or Ships of War in time of Peace, enter into any Agreement or Compact with another State, or with a foreign Power, or engage in War, unless actually invaded, or in such imminent Danger as will not admit of delay.

ARTICLE II.

Section. 1.

The executive Power shall be vested in a President of the United States of America. He shall hold his Office during the Term of four Years, and, together with the Vice President, chosen for the same Term, be elected, as follows:

Each State shall appoint, in such Manner as the Legislature thereof may direct, a Number of Electors, equal to the whole Number of Senators and Representatives to which the State may be entitled in the Congress: but no Senator or Representative, or Person holding an Office of Trust or Profit under the United States, shall be appointed an Elector.

The Electors shall meet in their respective States, and vote by Ballot for two Persons, of whom one at least shall not be an Inhabitant of the same State with themselves. And they shall make a List of all the Persons voted for, and of the Number of Votes for each; which List they shall sign and certify, and transmit sealed to the Seat of the Government of the United States, directed to the President of the Senate. The President of the Senate shall, in the Presence of the Senate and House of Representatives, open all the Certificates, and the Votes shall then be counted. The Person having the greatest Number of Votes shall be the President, if such Number be a Majority of the whole Number of Electors appointed; and if there be more than one who have such Majority, and have an equal Number of Votes, then the House of Representatives shall immediately chuse by Ballot one of them for President; and if no Person have a Majority, then from the five highest on the List the said House shall in like Manner chuse the President. But in chusing the President, the Votes shall be taken by States, the Representation from each State having one Vote; A quorum for this purpose shall consist of a Member or Members from two thirds of the States, and a Majority of all the States shall be necessary to a Choice. In every Case, after the Choice of the President, the Person having the greatest Number of Votes of the Electors shall be the Vice President. But if there should remain two or more who have equal Votes, the Senate shall chuse from them by Ballot the Vice President.

The Congress may determine the Time of chusing the Electors, and the Day on which they shall give their Votes; which Day shall be the same throughout the United States.

No Person except a natural born Citizen, or a Citizen of the United States, at the time of the Adoption of this Constitution, shall be eligible to the Office of President; neither shall any Person be eligible to that Office who shall not have attained to the Age of thirty five Years, and been fourteen Years a Resident within the United States.

In Case of the Removal of the President from Office, or of his Death, Resignation, or Inability to discharge the Powers and Duties of the said Office, the Same shall devolve on the Vice President, and the Congress may by Law provide for the Case of Removal, Death, Resignation or Inability, both of the President and Vice President, declaring what Officer shall then act as President, and such Officer shall act accordingly, until the Disability be removed, or a President shall be elected.

The President shall, at stated Times, receive for his Services, a Compensation, which shall neither be increased nor diminished during the Period for which he shall have been elected, and he shall not receive within that Period any other Emolument from the United States, or any of them.

Before he enter on the Execution of his Office, he shall take the following Oath or Affirmation:—"I do solemnly swear (or affirm) that I will faithfully execute the Office of President of the United States, and will to the best of my Ability, preserve, protect and defend the Constitution of the United States."

Section. 2.

The President shall be Commander in Chief of the Army and Navy of the United States, and of the Militia of the several States, when called into the actual Service of the United States; he may require the Opinion, in writing, of the principal Officer in each of the executive Departments, upon any Subject relating to the Duties of their respective Offices, and he shall have Power to grant Reprieves and Pardons for Offences against the United States, except in Cases of Impeachment.

He shall have Power, by and with the Advice and Consent of the Senate, to make Treaties, provided two thirds of the Senators present concur; and he shall nominate, and by and with the Advice and Consent of the Senate, shall appoint Ambassadors, other public Ministers and Consuls, Judges of the supreme Court, and all other Officers of the United States, whose Appointments are not herein otherwise provided for, and which shall be established by Law: but the Congress may by Law vest the Appointment of such inferior Officers, as they think proper, in the President alone, in the Courts of Law, or in the Heads of Departments.

The President shall have Power to fill up all Vacancies that may happen during the Recess of the Senate, by granting Commissions which shall expire at the End of their next Session.

Section. 3.

He shall from time to time give to the Congress Information of the State of the Union, and recommend to their Consideration such Measures as he shall judge necessary and expedient; he may, on extraordinary Occasions, convene both Houses, or either of them, and in Case of Disagreement between them, with Respect to the Time of Adjournment, he may adjourn them to such Time as he shall think proper; he shall receive Ambassadors and other public Ministers; he shall take Care that the Laws be faithfully executed, and shall Commission all the Officers of the United States.

Section. 4.

The President, Vice President and all civil Officers of the United States, shall be removed from Office on Impeachment for, and Conviction of, Treason, Bribery, or other high Crimes and Misdemeanors.

ARTICLE III.

Section. 1.

The judicial Power of the United States shall be vested in one supreme Court, and in such inferior Courts as the Congress may from time to time ordain and establish. The Judges, both of the supreme and inferior Courts, shall hold their Offices during good Behaviour, and shall, at stated Times, receive for their Services a Compensation, which shall not be diminished during their Continuance in Office.

Section. 2.
The judicial Power shall extend to all Cases, in Law and Equity, arising under this Constitution, the Laws of the United States, and Treaties made, or which shall be made, under their Authority;—to all Cases affecting Ambassadors, other public Ministers and Consuls;—to all Cases of admiralty and maritime Jurisdiction;—to Controversies to which the United States shall be a Party;—to Controversies between two or more States;—between a State and Citizens of another State,—between Citizens of different States,—between Citizens of the same State claiming Lands under Grants of different States, and between a State, or the Citizens thereof, and foreign States, Citizens or Subjects.

In all Cases affecting Ambassadors, other public Ministers and Consuls, and those in which a State shall be Party, the supreme Court shall have original Jurisdiction. In all the other Cases before mentioned, the supreme Court shall have appellate Jurisdiction, both as to Law and Fact, with such Exceptions, and under such Regulations as the Congress shall make.

The Trial of all Crimes, except in Cases of Impeachment, shall be by Jury; and such Trial shall be held in the State where the said Crimes shall have been committed; but when not committed within any State, the Trial shall be at such Place or Places as the Congress may by Law have directed.

Section. 3.
Treason against the United States, shall consist only in levying War against them, or in adhering to their Enemies, giving them Aid and Comfort. No Person shall be convicted of Treason unless on the Testimony of two Witnesses to the same overt Act, or on Confession in open Court.

The Congress shall have Power to declare the Punishment of Treason, but no Attainder of Treason shall work Corruption of Blood, or Forfeiture except during the Life of the Person attainted.

ARTICLE IV.
Section. 1.
Full Faith and Credit shall be given in each State to the public Acts, Records, and judicial Proceedings of every other State. And the Congress may by general Laws prescribe the Manner in which such Acts, Records and Proceedings shall be proved, and the Effect thereof.

Section. 2.
The Citizens of each State shall be entitled to all Privileges and Immunities of Citizens in the several States.

A Person charged in any State with Treason, Felony, or other Crime, who shall flee from Justice, and be found in another State, shall on Demand of the executive Authority of the State from which he fled, be delivered up, to be removed to the State having Jurisdiction of the Crime.

No Person held to Service or Labour in one State, under the Laws thereof, escaping into another, shall, in Consequence of any Law or Regulation therein, be discharged from such Service or Labour, but shall be delivered up on Claim of the Party to whom such Service or Labour may be due.

Section. 3.
New States may be admitted by the Congress into this Union; but no new State shall be formed or erected within the Jurisdiction of any other State; nor any State be formed by the Junction of two or more States, or Parts of States, without the Consent of the Legislatures of the States concerned as well as of the Congress.

The Congress shall have Power to dispose of and make all needful Rules and Regulations respecting the Territory or other Property belonging to the United States; and nothing in this Constitution shall be so construed as to Prejudice any Claims of the United States, or of any particular State.

Section. 4.
The United States shall guarantee to every State in this Union a Republican Form of Government, and shall protect each of them against Invasion; and on Application of the Legislature, or of the Executive (when the Legislature cannot be convened), against domestic Violence.

ARTICLE V.

The Congress, whenever two thirds of both Houses shall deem it necessary, shall propose Amendments to this Constitution, or, on the Application of the Legislatures of two thirds of the several States, shall call a Convention for proposing Amendments, which, in either Case, shall be valid to all Intents and Purposes, as Part of this Constitution, when ratified by the Legislatures of three fourths of the several States, or by Conventions in three fourths thereof, as the one or the other Mode of Ratification may be proposed by the Congress; Provided that no Amendment which may be made prior to the Year One thousand eight hundred and eight shall in any Manner affect the first and fourth Clauses in the Ninth Section of the first Article; and that no State, without its Consent, shall be deprived of its equal Suffrage in the Senate.

ARTICLE VI.

All Debts contracted and Engagements entered into, before the Adoption of this Constitution, shall be as valid against the United States under this Constitution, as under the Confederation.

This Constitution, and the Laws of the United States which shall be made in Pursuance thereof; and all Treaties made, or which shall be made, under the Authority of the United States, shall be the supreme Law of the Land; and the Judges in every State shall be bound thereby, any Thing in the Constitution or Laws of any State to the Contrary notwithstanding.

The Senators and Representatives before mentioned, and the Members of the several State Legislatures, and all executive and judicial Officers, both of the United States and of the several States, shall be bound by Oath or Affirmation, to support this Constitution; but no religious Test shall ever be required as a Qualification to any Office or public Trust under the United States.

ARTICLE VII.

The Ratification of the Conventions of nine States, shall be sufficient for the Establishment of this Constitution between the States so ratifying the Same.

The Word, "the," being interlined between the seventh and eighth Lines of the first Page, the Word "Thirty" being partly written on an Erazure in the fifteenth Line of the first Page, The Words "is tried" being interlined between the thirty second and thirty third Lines of the first Page and the Word "the" being interlined between the forty third and forty fourth Lines of the second Page.

DRAWING CONCLUSIONS:

1. Explain, in your own words, the key provisions of the Constitution.
   a. The method for choosing members of the three branches.
   b. The powers of each branch.
   c. Limits on the powers of the three branches.
   d. Limits on the powers of the state governments.
2. What are a few key provisions of the Constitution that were democratic? (In other words, which provisions grant power to ordinary people to govern themselves?)
3. What are a few key provisions of the Constitution that were undemocratic? (In other words, which provisions place limits on the ability of ordinary people to govern themselves?)

1.4 THE CONSTITUTIONS OF VIRGINIA (1776) AND PENNSYLVANIA (1776)

The US Constitution can also be evaluated by contrasting it with state constitutions that preceded it. Two state constitutions (those of Virginia and Pennsylvania) are presented here. As you examine these documents, look for ways that each constitution is similar to or differs from the federal constitution that emerged from the 1787 Philadelphia convention. In what ways, if any, were these state constitutions more or less democratic than the federal constitution that followed?

When reading the Virginia constitution, you will note that it states that the right to suffrage (i.e., the right to vote) would remain as it was. At the time that the Virginia constitution was adopted, the state law limited the right to vote on the basis of property ownership, sex, and race.

GUIDING QUESTIONS:

1. For each state constitution, identify ways in which it was similar to or different from the United States Constitution as originally drafted in 1787. Think about
   a. The method for choosing members of the three branches
   b. The powers of each branch
   c. Limits on the powers of the three branches
   d. Specific protections for individual rights

THE CONSTITUTION OF VIRGINIA—1776

BILL OF RIGHTS

A declaration of rights made by the representatives of the good people of Virginia, assembled in full and free convention; which rights do pertain to them and their posterity, as the basis and foundation of government.

SECTION 1. That all men are by nature equally free and independent, and have certain inherent rights, of which, when they enter into a state of society, they cannot, by any compact, deprive or divest their posterity, namely, the enjoyment of life and liberty, with the means of acquiring and possessing property, and pursuing and obtaining happiness and safety.

SEC. 2. That all power is vested in, and consequently derived from, the people; that magistrates are their trustees and servants, and at all times amenable to them.

SEC. 3. That government is, or ought to be, instituted for the common benefit, protection, and security of the people, nation, or community; of all the various modes and forms of government, that is best which is capable of producing the greatest degree of happiness and safety, and is most effectually secured against the danger of maladministration; and that, when any government shall be found inadequate or contrary to these purposes, a majority of the community hath an indubitable, inalienable, and indefeasible right to reform, alter, or abolish it, in such manner as shall be judged most conducive to the public weal.

SEC. 4. That no man, or set of men, are entitled to exclusive or separate emoluments or privileges from the community, but in consideration of public services; which, not being descendible, neither ought the offices of magistrate, legislator, or judge to be hereditary.

Francis Newton Thorpe, ed, *The Federal and State Constitutions Colonial Charters, and Other Organic Laws of the States, Territories, and Colonies Now or Heretofore Forming the United States of America* (Washington, DC: Government Printing Office, 1909), Volume 7, pp. 3812–3819.

SEC. 5. That the legislative and executive powers of the State should be separate and distinct from the judiciary; and that the members of the two first may be restrained from oppression, by feeling and participating the burdens of the people, they should, at fixed periods, be reduced to a private station, return into that body from which they were originally taken, and the vacancies be supplied by frequent, certain, and regular elections, in which all, or any part of the former members, to be again eligible, or ineligible, as the laws shall direct.

SEC. 6. That elections of members to serve as representatives of the people, in assembly, ought to be free; and that all men, having sufficient evidence of permanent common interest with, and attachment to, the community, have the right of suffrage, and cannot be taxed or deprived of their property for public uses, without their own consent, or that of their representatives so elected, nor bound by any law to which they have not, in like manner, assembled, for the public good.

SEC. 7. That all power of suspending laws, or the execution of laws, by any authority, without consent of the representatives of the people, is injurious to their rights, and ought not to be exercised.

SEC. 8. That in all capital or criminal prosecutions a man hath a right to demand the cause and nature of his accusation, to be confronted with the accusers and witnesses, to call for evidence in his favor, and to a speedy trial by an impartial jury of twelve men of his vicinage, without whose unanimous consent he cannot be found guilty; nor can he be compelled to give evidence against himself; that no man be deprived of his liberty, except by the law of the land or the judgment of his peers.

SEC. 9. That excessive bail ought not to be required, nor excessive fines imposed, nor cruel and unusual punishments inflicted.

SEC. 10. That general warrants, whereby an officer or messenger may be commanded to search suspected places without evidence of a fact committed, or to seize any person or persons not named, or whose offence is not particularly described and supported by evidence, are grievous and oppressive, and ought not to be granted.

SEC. 11. That in controversies respecting property, and in suits between man and man, the ancient trial by jury is preferable to any other, and ought to be held sacred.

SEC. 12. That the freedom of the press is one of the great bulwarks of liberty, and can never be restrained but by despotic governments.

SEC. 13. That a well-regulated militia, composed of the body of the people, trained to arms, is the proper, natural, and safe defence of a free State; that standing armies, in time of peace, should be avoided, as dangerous to liberty; and that in all cases the military should be under strict subordination to, and governed by, the civil power.

SEC. 14. That the people have a right to uniform government; and, therefore, that no government separate from, or independent of the government of Virginia, ought to be erected or established within the limits thereof.

SEC. 15. That no free government, or the blessings of liberty, can be preserved to any people, but by a firm adherence to justice, moderation, temperance, frugality, and virtue, and by frequent recurrence to fundamental principles.

SEC. 16. That religion, or the duty which we owe to our Creator, and the manner of discharging it, can be directed only by reason and conviction, not by force or violence; and therefore all men are equally entitled to the free exercise of religion, according to the dictates of conscience; and that it is the mutual duty of all to practice Christian forbearance, love, and charity towards each other.

THE CONSTITUTION OR FORM OF GOVERNMENT, AGREED TO AND RESOLVED UPON BY THE DELEGATES AND REPRESENTATIVES OF THE SEVERAL COUNTIES AND CORPORATIONS OF VIRGINIA

Whereas George the third, King of Great Britain and Ireland, and elector of Hanover, heretofore intrusted with the exercise of the kingly office in this government, hath endeavoured to prevent, the same into a detestable and insupportable tyranny, by putting his negative on laws the most wholesome and necessary for the public good:

By denying his Governors permission to pass laws of immediate and pressing importance, unless suspended in their operation for his assent, and, when so suspended neglecting to attend to them for many years:

By refusing to pass certain other laws, unless the persons to be benefited by them would relinquish the inestimable right of representation in the legislature:

By dissolving legislative Assemblies repeatedly and continually, for opposing with manly firmness his invasions of the rights of the people:

When dissolved, by refusing to call others for a long space of time, thereby leaving the political system without any legislative head:

By endeavouring to prevent the population of our country, and, for that purpose, obstructing, the laws for the naturalization of foreigners:

By keeping among us, in times of peace, standing armies and ships of war:

By effecting to render the military independent of, and superior to, the civil power:

By combining with others to subject us to a foreign jurisdiction, giving his assent to their pretended acts of legislation:

For quartering large bodies of armed troops among us:

For cutting off our trade with all parts of the world:

For imposing taxes on us without our consent:

For depriving us of the benefits of trial by jury:

For transporting us beyond seas, to be tried for pretended offences:

For suspending our own legislatures, and declaring themselves invested with power to legislate for us in all cases whatsoever:

By plundering our seas, ravaging our coasts, burning our towns, and destroying the lives of our people:

By inciting insurrections of our fellow subjects, with the allurements of forfeiture and confiscation:

By prompting our negroes to rise in arms against us, those very negroes whom, by an inhuman use of his negative, he hath refused us permission to exclude by law:

By endeavoring to bring on the inhabitants of our frontiers the merciless Indian savages, whose known rule of warfare is an undistinguished destruction of all ages, sexes, and conditions of existence:

By transporting, at this time, a large army of foreign mercenaries, to complete the works of death, desolation, and tyranny, already begun with circumstances of cruelty and perfidy unworthy the head of a civilized nation:

By answering our repeated petitions for redress with a repetition of injuries: And finally, by abandoning the helm of government and declaring us out of his allegiance and protection.

By which several acts of misrule, the government of this country, as formerly exercised under the crown of Great Britain, is TOTALLY DISSOLVED.

We therefore, the delegates and representatives of the good people of Virginia, having maturely considered the premises, and viewing with great concern the deplorable conditions to which this once happy country must be reduced, unless some regular, adequate mode of civil polity is speedily adopted, and in compliance with a recommendation of the General Congress, do ordain and declare the future form of government of Virginia to be as followeth:

The legislative, executive, and judiciary department, shall be separate and distinct, so that neither exercise the powers properly belonging to the other: nor shall any person exercise the powers of more than one of them, at the same time; except that the Justices of the County Courts shall be eligible to either House of Assembly.

The legislative shall be formed of two distinct branches, who, together, shall be a complete Legislature. They shall meet once, or oftener, every year, and shall be called, The General Assembly of Virginia. One of these shall be called, The House of Delegates, and consist of two Representatives, to be chosen for each county, and for the district of West Augusta, annually, of such men as actually reside in, and are freeholders of the same, or duly qualified according to law, and also of one Delegate or Representative, to be chosen annually for the city of Williamsburgh, and one for the borough of Norfolk, and a Representative for each of such other cities and boroughs, as may hereafter be allowed particular representation by the legislature; but when any city or borough shall so decrease, as that the number of persons, having right of suffrage therein, shall have been, for the space of seven Years successively, less than half the number of voters in some one county in Virginia, such city or borough thenceforward shall cease to send a Delegate or Representative to the Assembly.

The other shall be called The Senate, and consist of twenty-four members, of whom thirteen shall constitute a House to proceed on business; for whose election, the different counties shall be divided into twenty-four districts; and each county of the respective district, at the time of the election of its Delegates, shall vote for one Senator, who is actually a resident and freeholder within the district, or duly qualified according to law, and is upwards of twenty-five years of age; and the Sheriffs of each county, within five days at farthest, after the last county election in the district, shall meet at some convenient place, and from the poll, so taken in their respective counties, return, as a Senator, the man who shall have the greatest number of votes in the whole district. To keep up this Assembly by rotation, the districts shall be equally divided into four classes and numbered by lot. At the end of one year after the general election, the six members, elected by the first division, shall be displaced, and the vacancies thereby occasioned supplied from such class or division, by new election, in the manner aforesaid. This rotation shall be applied to each division, according to its number, and continued in due order annually.

The right of suffrage in the election of members for both Houses shall remain as exercised at present; and each House shall choose its own Speaker, appoint its own officers, settle its own rules of proceeding, and direct writs of election, for the supplying intermediate vacancies.

All laws shall originate in the House of Delegates, to be approved of or rejected by the Senate, or to be amended, with consent of the House of Delegates; except money bills, which in no instance shall be altered by the Senate, but wholly approved or rejected.

A Governor, or chief magistrate, shall be chosen annually by joint ballot of both Houses (to be taken in each House respectively) deposited in the conference room; the boxes examined jointly by a committee of each House, and the numbers severally reported to them, that the appointments may be entered (which shall be the mode of taking the joint ballot of both Houses, in all cases) who shall not continue in that office longer than three years successively. nor be eligible, until the expiration of four years after he shall have been out of that office. An adequate, but moderate salary shall be settled on him, during his continuance in office; and he shall, with the advice of a Council of State, exercise the executive powers of government, according to the laws of this Commonwealth; and shall not, under any presence, exercise any power or prerogative, by virtue of any law, statute or custom of England. But he shall, with the advice of the Council of State, have the power of granting reprieves or pardons, except where the prosecution shall have been carried on by the House of Delegates, or the law shall otherwise particularly direct: in which cases, no reprieve or pardon shall be granted, but by resolve of the House of Delegates.

Either House of the General Assembly may adjourn themselves respectively. The Governor shall not prorogue or adjourn the Assembly, during their sitting, nor dissolve them at any time; but he shall, if necessary, either by advice of the Council of State, or on application of a majority of the House of Delegates, call them before the time to which they shall stand prorogued or adjourned.

A Privy Council, or Council of State, consisting of eight members, shall be chosen, by joint ballot of both Houses of Assembly, either from their own members or the people at large, to assist in the administration of government. They shall annually choose, out of their own members, a President, who, in case of death, inability, or absence of the Governor from the government, shall act as Lieutenant Governor. Four members shall be sufficient to act, and their advice and proceedings shall be entered on record, and signed by the members present, (to any part whereof, any member may enter his dissent) to be laid before the General Assembly, when called for by them. This Council may appoint their own Clerk, who shall have a salary settled by law, and take an oath of secrecy, in such matters as he shall be directed by the board to conceal. A sum of money, appropriated to that purpose, shall be divided annually among the members in proportion to their attendance; and they shall be incapable, during their continuance in office, of sitting in either House of Assembly. Two members shall be removed, by Joint ballot of both Houses of

Assembly, at the end of every three years, and be ineligible for the three next years. These vacancies, as well as those occasioned by death or incapacity, shall be supplied by new elections, in the same manner.

The Delegates for Virginia to the Continental Congress shall be chosen annually, or superseded in the mean time, by joint ballot of both Houses of Assembly.

The present militia officers shall be continued, and vacancies supplied by appointment of the Governor, with the advice of the Privy Council, on recommendations from the respective County Courts; but the Governor and Council shall have a power of suspending any officer, and ordering a Court Martial, on complaint of misbehaviour or inability, or to supply vacancies of officers, happening when in actual service.

The Governor may embody the militia, with the advice of the Privy Council; and when embodied, shall alone have the direction of the militia, under the laws of the country.

The two Houses of Assembly shall, by joint ballot, appoint Judges of the Supreme Court of Appeals, and General Court, Judges in Chancery, Judges of Admiralty, Secretary, and the Attorney General, to be commissioned by the Governor, and continue in office during good behaviour. In case of death, incapacity, or resignation, the Governor, with the advice of the Privy Council, shall appoint persons to succeed in office, to be approved or displaced by both Houses. These officers shall have fixed and adequate salaries, and, together with all others, holding lucrative offices, and all ministers of the gospel, of every denomination, be incapable of being elected members of either House of Assembly or the Privy Council.

The Governor, with the advice of the Privy Council, shall appoint Justices of the Peace for the counties; and in case of vacancies, or a necessity of increasing the number hereafter, such appointments to be made upon the recommendation of the respective County Courts. The present acting Secretary in Virginia, and Clerks of all the County Courts, shall continue in office. In case of vacancies, either by death, incapacity, or resignation, a Secretary shall be appointed, as before directed; and the Clerks, by the respective Courts. The present and future Clerks shall hold their offices during good behaviour, to be judged of, and determined in the General Court. The Sheriffs and Coroners shall be nominated by the respective Courts, approved by the Governor, with the advice of the Privy Council, and commissioned by the Governor. The Justices shall appoint Constables; and all fees of the aforesaid officers be regulated by law.

The Governor, when he is out of office, and others, offending against the State, either by mal-administration, corruption, or other means, by which the safety of the State may be endangered, shall be impeachable by the House of Delegates. Such impeachment to be prosecuted by the Attorney General, or such other person or persons, as the House may appoint in the General Court, according to the laws of the land. If found guilty, he or they shall be either forever disabled to hold any office under government, or be removed from such office pro tempore, or subjected to such pains or penalties as the laws shall direct.

If all or any of the Judges of the General Court should on good grounds (to be judged of by the House of Delegates) be accused of any of the crimes or offences above mentioned, such House of Delegates may, in like manner, impeach the Judge or Judges so accused, to be prosecuted in the Court of Appeals; and he or they, if found guilty, shall be punished in the same manner as is prescribed in the preceding clause.

Commissions and grants shall run, "In the name of the Commonwealth of Virginia," and bear test by the Governor, with the seal of the Commonwealth annexed. Writs shall run in the same manner, and bear test by the Clerks of the several Courts. Indictments shall conclude, "Against the peace and dignity of the Commonwealth."

A Treasurer shall be appointed annually, by joint ballot of both Houses.

All escheats, penalties, and forfeitures, heretofore going to the King, shall go to the Commonwealth, save only such as the Legislature may abolish, or otherwise provide for.

The territories, contained within the Charters, erecting the Colonies of Maryland, Pennsylvania, North and South Carolina, are hereby ceded, released, and forever confirmed, to the people of these Colonies respectively, with all the rights of property, jurisdiction and government, and all other rights whatsoever, which might, at any time heretofore, have been claimed by Virginia, except the free navigation and use of the rivers Patomaque and Pokomoke, with the property of the Virginia shores and strands, bordering on either of the said rivers, and all improvements, which have been, or shall be made thereon. The western and northern extent of Virginia shall, in all other respects, stand as fixed by the Charter of King James I. in the year one thousand six hundred and nine, and by the public treaty of peace between the Courts of Britain and France, in the Year one thousand seven hundred and sixty-three; unless by act of this Legislature, one or more governments be established westward of the Alleghany mountains. And no purchases of lands shall be made of the Indian natives, but on behalf of the public, by authority of the General Assembly.

In order to introduce this government, the Representatives of the people met in the convention shall choose a Governor and Privy Council, also such other officers directed to be chosen by both Houses as may be judged necessary to be immediately appointed. The Senate to be first chosen by the people to continue until the last day of March next, and the other officers until the end of the succeeding session of Assembly. In case of vacancies, the Speaker of either House shall issue writs for new elections.

CONSTITUTION OF PENNSYLVANIA—1776

WHEREAS all government ought to be instituted and supported for the security and protection of the community as such, and to enable the individuals who compose it to enjoy their natural rights, and the other blessings which the Author of existence has bestowed upon man; and whenever these great ends of government are not obtained, the people have a right, by common consent to change it, and take such measures as to them may appear necessary to promote their safety and happiness. AND WHEREAS the inhabitants of this commonwealth have in consideration of

protection only, heretofore acknowledged allegiance to the king of Great Britain; and the said king has not only withdrawn that protection, but commenced, and still continues to carry on, with unabated vengeance, a most cruel and unjust war against them, employing therein, not only the troops of Great Britain, but foreign mercenaries, savages and slaves, for the avowed purpose of reducing them to a total and abject submission to the despotic domination of the British parliament, with many other acts of tyranny, (more fully set forth in the declaration of Congress) whereby all allegiance and fealty to the said king and his successors, are dissolved and at an end, and all power and authority derived from him ceased in these colonies. AND WHEREAS it is absolutely necessary for the welfare and safety of the inhabitants of said colonies, that they be henceforth free and independent States, and that just, permanent, and proper forms of government exist in every part of them, derived from and founded on the authority of the people only, agreeable to the directions of the honourable American Congress. We, the representatives of the freemen of Pennsylvania, in general convention met, for the express purpose of framing such a government, confessing the goodness of the great Governor of the universe (who alone knows to what degree of earthly happiness mankind may attain, by perfecting the arts of government) in permitting the people of this State, by common consent, and without violence, deliberately to form for themselves such just rules as they shall think best, for governing their future society, and being fully convinced, that it is our indispensable duty to establish such original principles of government, as will best promote the general happiness of the people of this State, and their posterity, and provide for future improvements, without partiality for, or prejudice against any particular class, sect, or denomination of men whatever, do, by virtue of the authority vested in use by our constituents, ordain, declare, and establish, the following Declaration of Rights and Frame of Government, to be the CONSTITUTION of this commonwealth, and to remain in force therein for ever,

Francis Newton Thorpe, ed, *The Federal and State Constitutions Colonial Charters, and Other Organic Laws of the States, Territories, and Colonies Now or Heretofore Forming the United States of America* (Washington, DC: Government Printing Office, 1909), Volume 5, pp. 3081–3092.

unaltered, except in such articles as shall hereafter on experience be found to require improvement, and which shall by the same authority of the people, fairly delegated as this frame of government directs, be amended or improved for the more effectual obtaining and securing the great end and design of all government, herein before mentioned.

A DECLARATION OF THE RIGHTS OF THE INHABITANTS OF THE COMMONWEALTH OR STATE OF PENNSYLVANIA

I. That all men are born equally free and independent, and have certain natural, inherent and inalienable rights, amongst which are, the enjoying and defending life and liberty, acquiring, possessing and protecting property, and pursuing and obtaining happiness and safety.

II. That all men have a natural and unalienable right to worship Almighty God according to the dictates of their own consciences and understanding: And that no man ought or of right can be compelled to attend any religious worship, or erect or support any place of worship, or maintain any ministry, contrary to, or against, his own free will and consent: Nor can any man, who acknowledges the being of a God, be justly deprived or abridged of any civil right as a citizen, on account of his religious sentiments or peculiar mode of religious worship: And that no authority can or ought to be vested in, or assumed by any power whatever, that shall in any case interfere with, or in any manner controul, the right of conscience in the free exercise of religious worship.

III. That the people of this State have the sole, exclusive and inherent right of governing and regulating the internal police of the same.

IV. That all power being originally inherent in, and consequently derived from, the people; therefore all officers of government, whether legislative or executive, are their trustees and servants, and at all times accountable to them.

V. That government is, or ought to be, instituted for the common benefit, protection and security of the people, nation or community; and not for the particular emolument or advantage of any single man, family, or soft of men, who are a part only of that community, And that the community hath an indubitable, unalienable and indefeasible right to reform, alter, or abolish government in such manner as shall be by that community judged most conducive to the public weal.

VI. That those who are employed in the legislative and executive business of the State, may be restrained from oppression, the people have a right, at such periods as they may think proper, to reduce their public officers to a private station, and supply the vacancies by certain and regular elections.

VII. That all elections ought to be free; and that all free men having a sufficient evident common interest with, and attachment to the community, have a right to elect officers, or to be elected into office.

VIII. That every member of society hath a right to be protected in the enjoyment of life, liberty and property, and therefore is bound to contribute his proportion towards the expence of that protection, and yield his personal service when necessary, or an equivalent thereto: But no part of a man's property can be justly taken from him, or applied to public uses, without his own consent, or that of his legal representatives: Nor can any man who is conscientiously scrupulous of bearing arms, be justly compelled thereto, if he will pay such equivalent, nor are the people bound by any laws, but such as they have in like manner assented to, for their common good.

IX. That in all prosecutions for criminal offences, a man hath a right to be heard by himself and his council, to demand the cause and nature of his accusation, to be confronted with the witnesses, to call for evidence in his favour, and a speedy public trial, by an impartial jury of the country, without the unanimous consent of which jury he cannot be found guilty; nor can he be compelled to give evidence against himself; nor can any man be justly deprived of his liberty except by the laws of the land, or the judgment of his peers.

X. That the people have a right to hold themselves, their houses, papers, and possessions free from search and seizure, and therefore warrants without oaths or affirmations first made, affording a sufficient foundation for them, and whereby any officer or messenger may be commanded or required to search suspected places, or to seize any person or persons, his or their property, not particularly described, are contrary to that right, and ought not to be granted.

XI. That in controversies respecting property, and in suits between man and man, the parties have a right to trial by jury, which ought to be held sacred.

XII. That the people have a right to freedom of speech, and of writing, and publishing their sentiments; therefore the freedom of the press ought not to be restrained.

XIII. That the people have a right to bear arms for the defence of themselves and the state; and as standing armies in the time of peace are dangerous to liberty, they ought not to be kept up; And that the military should be kept under strict subordination to, and governed by, the civil power.

XIV. That a frequent recurrence to fundamental principles, and a firm adherence to justice, moderation, temperance, industry, and frugality are absolutely necessary to preserve the blessings of liberty, and keep a government free: The people ought therefore to pay particular attention to these points in the choice of officers and representatives, and have a right to exact a due and constant regard to them, from their legislatures and magistrates, in the making and executing such laws as are necessary for the good government of the state.

XV. That all men have a natural inherent right to emigrate from one state to another that will receive them, or to form a new state in vacant countries, or in such countries as they can purchase, whenever they think that thereby they may promote their own happiness.

XVI. That the people have a right to assemble together, to consult for their common good, to instruct their representatives, and to apply to the legislature for redress of grievances, by address, petition, or remonstrance.

PLAN OR FRAME OF GOVERNMENT FOR THE COMMONWEALTH OR STATE OF PENNSYLVANIA

SECTION 1. The commonwealth or state of Pennsylvania shall be governed hereafter by an assembly of the representatives of the freemen of the same, and a president and council, in manner and form following–

SECT. 2. The supreme legislative power shall be vested in a house of representatives of the freemen of the commonwealth or state of Pennsylvania.

SECT. 3. The supreme executive power shall be vested in a president and council.

SECT. 4. Courts of justice shall be established in the city of Philadelphia, and in every county of this state.

SECT. 5. The freemen of this commonwealth and their sons shall be trained and armed for its defence under such regulations, restrictions, and exceptions as the general assembly shall by law direct, preserving always to the people the right of choosing their colonels and all commissioned officers under that rank, in such manner and as often as by the said laws shall be directed.

SECT. 6. Every freemen of the full age of twenty-one Years, having resided in this state for the space of one whole Year next before the day of election for representatives, and paid public taxes during that time, shall enjoy the right of an elector: Provided always, that sons of freeholders of the age of twenty-one years shall be intitled to vote although they have not paid taxes.

SECT. 7. The house of representatives of the freemen of this commonwealth shall consist of persons most noted for wisdom and virtue, to be chosen by the freemen of every city and county of this commonwealth respectively. And no person shall be elected unless he has resided in the city or county for which he shall be chosen two years immediately before the said election; nor shall any member, while he continues such, hold any other office, except in the militia.

SECT. 8. No person shall be capable of being elected a member to serve in the house of representatives of the freemen of this commonwealth more than four years in seven.

SECT. 9. The members of the house of representatives shall be chosen annually by ballot, by the freemen of the commonwealth, on the second Tuesday in October forever, (except this present year,) and shall meet on the fourth Monday of the same month, and shall be stiled, The general assembly of the representatives of the freemen of Pennsylvania, and shall have power to choose their speaker, the treasurer of the state, and their other officers; sit on their own adjournments; prepare bills and enact them into laws; judge of the elections and qualifications of their own members; they may expel a member, but not a second time for the same cause; they may administer oaths or affirmations on examination of witnesses; redress grievances; impeach state criminals; grant charters of incorporation; constitute towns, boroughs, cities, and counties; and shall have all other powers necessary for the legislature of a free state or commonwealth: But they shall have no power to add to, alter, abolish, or infringe any part of this constitution.

SECT. 10. A quorum of the house of representatives shall consist of two-thirds of the whole number of members elected; and having met and chosen their speaker, shall each of them before they proceed to business take and subscribe, as well the oath or affirmation of fidelity and allegiance hereinafter directed, as the following oath or affirmation, viz:

I do swear (or affirm) that as a member of this assembly, I will not propose or assent to any bill, vote, or resolution, which stall appear to free injurious to the people; nor do or consent to any act or thing whatever, that shall have a tendency to lessen or abridge their rights and privileges, as declared in the constitution of this state; but will in all things conduct myself as a faithful honest representative and guardian of the people, according to the best of only judgment and abilities.

And each member, before he takes his seat, shall make and subscribe the following declaration, viz:

I do believe in one God, the creator and governor of the universe, the rewarder of the good and the punisher of the wicked. And I do acknowledge the Scriptures of the Old and New Testament to be given by Divine inspiration.

And no further or other religious test shall ever hereafter be required of any civil officer or magistrate in this State.

SECT. 11. Delegates to represent this state in congress shall be chosen by ballot by the future general assembly at their first meeting, and annually forever afterwards, as long as such representation shall be necessary. Any delegate may be superseded at any time, by the general assembly appointing another in his stead. No man shall sit in congress longer than two years successively, nor be capable of reelection for three Years afterwards: and no person who holds any office in the gift of the congress shall hereafter be elected to represent this commonwealth in congress.

SECT. 12. If any city or cities, county or counties shall neglect or refuse to elect and send representatives to the general assembly, two-thirds of the members from the cities or counties that do elect and send representatives, provided they be a majority of the cities and counties of the whole state, when met, shall have all the powers of the general assembly, as fully and amply as if the whole were present.

SECT. 13. The doors of the house in which the representatives of the freemen of this state shall sit in general assembly, shall be and remain open for the admission of all persons who behave decently, except only when the welfare of this state may require the doors to be shut.

SECT. 14. The votes and proceedings of the general assembly shall be printed weekly during their sitting, with the yeas and nays, on any question, vote or resolution, where any two members require it except when the vote is taken by ballot; and when the yeas and nays are so taken every member shall have a right to insert the reasons of his vote upon the minutes, if he desires it.

SECT. 15. To the end that laws before they are enacted may be more maturely considered, and the inconvenience of hasty determinations as much as possible prevented, all bills of public nature shall be printed for the consideration of the people, before they are read in general assembly the last time for debate and amendment; and, except on occasions of sudden necessity, shall not be passed into laws until the next session of assembly; and for the more perfect satisfaction of the public, the reasons and motives for making such laws shall be fully and clearly expressed in the preambles.

SECT. 16. The stile of the laws of this commonwealth shall be, "Be it enacted, and it is hereby enacted by the representatives of the freemen of the commonwealth of Pennsylvania in general assembly met, and by the authority of the same." And the general assembly shall affix their seal to every bill, as soon as it is enacted into a law, which seal shall be kept by the assembly, and shall be called, The seal of the laws of Pennsylvania, and shall not be used for any other purpose.

SECT. 17. The city of Philadelphia and each county of this commonwealth respectively, shall on the first Tuesday of November in this present year, and on the second Tuesday of October annually for the two next succeeding years, viz. the year one thousand seven hundred and seventy-seven, and the year one thousand seven hundred and seventy-eight, choose six persons to represent them in general assembly. But as representation in proportion to the number of taxable inhabitants is the only principle which can at all times secure liberty, and make the voice of a majority of the people the law of the land; therefore the general assembly shall cause complete lists of the taxable inhabitants in the city and each county in the commonwealth respectively, to be taken and returned to them, on or before the last meeting of the assembly elected in the year one thousand seven hundred and seventy-eight, who shall appoint a representation to each, in proportion to the number of taxables in such returns; which representation shall continue for the next seven years afterwards at the end of which, a new return of the taxable inhabitants shall be made, and a representation agreeable thereto appointed by the said assembly, and so on septennially forever. The wages of the representatives in general assembly, and all other state charges shall be paid out of the state treasury.

SECT. 18. In order that the freemen of this commonwealth may enjoy the benefit of election as equally as may be until the representation shall commences as directed in the foregoing section, each county at its own choice may be divided into districts, hold elections therein, and elect their representatives in the county, and their other elective officers, as shall be hereafter regulated by the general assembly of this state. And no inhabitant of this state shall have more than one annual vote at the general election for representatives in assembly.

SECT. 19. For the present the supreme. executive council of this state shall consist of twelve persons chosen in the following manner: The freemen of the city of Philadelphia, and of the counties of Philadelphia, Chester, and Bucks, respectively, shall choose by ballot one person for the city, and one for each county aforesaid to serve for three years and no

longer, at the time and place for electing representatives in general assembly. The freemen of the counties of Lancaster, York, Cumberland, and Berks, shall, in like manner elect one person for each county respectively, to serve as counsellors for two years and no longer. And the counties of Northampton, Bedford, Northumberland and Westmoreland, respectively, shall, in like manner, elect one person for each county, to serve as counsellors for one year, and no longer. And at the expiration of the time for which each counsellor was chosen to serve, the freemen of the city of Philadelphia, and of the several counties in this state, respectively, shall elect one person to serve as counsellor for three years and no longer; and so on every third year forever. By this mode of election and continual rotation, more men will be trained to public business, there will in every subsequent year be found in the council a number of persons acquainted with the proceedings of the foregoing Years, whereby the business will be more consistently conducted, and moreover the danger of establishing an inconvenient aristocracy will be effectually prevented. All vacancies in the council that may happen by death, resignation, or otherwise, shall be filled at the next general election for representatives in general assembly, unless a particular election for that purpose shall be sooner appointed by the president and council. No member of the general assembly or delegate in congress, shall be chosen a member of the council. The president and vice-president shall be chosen annually by the joint ballot of the general assembly and council, of the members of the council. Any person having served as a counsellor for three successive years, shall be incapable of holding that office for four years afterwards. Every member of the council shall be a justice of the peace for the whole commonwealth, by virtue of his office.

In case new additional counties shall hereafter be erected in this state, such county or counties shall elect a counsellor, and such county or counties shall be annexed to the next neighbouring counties, and shall take rotation with such counties.

The council shall meet annually, at the same time and place with the general assembly.

The treasurer of the state, trustees of the loan office, naval officers, collectors of customs or excise, judge of the admirality, attornies general, sheriffs, and prothonotaries, shall not be capable of a seat in the general assembly, executive council, or continental congress.

SECT. 20. The president, and in his absence the vice-president, with the council, five of whom shall be a quorum, shall have power to appoint and commissionate judges, naval officers, judge of the admiralty, attorney general and all other officers, civil and military, except such as are chosen by the general assembly or the people, agreeable to this frame of government, and the laws that may be made hereafter; and shall supply every vacancy in any office, occasioned by death, resignation, removal or disqualification, until the office can be filled in the time and manner directed by law or this constitution. They are to correspond with other states, and transact business with the officers of government, civil and military; and to prepare such business as may appear to them necessary to lay before the general assembly. They shall sit as judges, to hear and determine on impeachments, taking to their assistance for advice only, the justices of the supreme court. And shall have power to grant pardons and remit fines, in all cases whatsoever, except in cases of impeachment; and in cases of treason and murder, shall have power to grant reprieves, but not to pardon, until the end of the next sessions of assembly; but there shall be no remission or mitigation of punishments on impeachments, except by act of the legislature; they are also to take care that the laws be faithfully executed; they are to expedite the execution of such measures as may be resolved upon by the general assembly; and they may draw upon the treasury for such sums as shall be appropriated by the house: They may also lay embargoes, or prohibit the exportation of any commodity, for any time, not exceeding thirty days, in the recess of the house only: They may grant such licences, as shall be directed by law, and shall have power to call together the general assembly when necessary, before the day to which they shall stand adjourned. The president shall be commander in chief of the forces of the state, but shall not command in person, except advised thereto by the council, and then only so long as they shall approve thereof. The president and council shall have a secretary, and keep fair books of

their proceedings, wherein any counsellor may enter his dissent, with his reasons in support of it.

SECT. 21. All commissions shall be in the name, and by the authority of the freemen of the commonwealth of Pennsylvania, sealed with the state seal, signed by the president or vice-president, and attested by the secretary; which seal shall be kept by the council.

SECT. 22. Every officer of state, whether judicial or executive, shall be liable to be impeached by the general assembly, either when in office, or after his resignation or removal for mal-administration: All impeachments shall be before the president or vice-president and council, who shall hear and determine the same.

SECT. 23. The judges of the supreme court of judicature shall have fixed salaries, be commissioned for seven years only, though capable of re-appointment at the end of that term, but removable for misbehaviour at any time by the general assembly; they shall not be allowed to sit as members in the continental congress, executive council, or general assembly, nor to hold any other office civil or military, nor to take or receive fees or perquisites of any kind.

SECT. 24. The supreme court, and the several courts of common pleas of this commonwealth, shall, besides the powers usually exercised by such courts, have the powers of a court of chancery, so far as relates to the perpetuating testimony, obtaining evidence from places not within this state, and the care of the persons and estates of those who are non compotes mentis, and such other powers as may be found necessary by future general assemblies, not inconsistent with this constitution.

SECT. 25. Trials shall be by jury as heretofore: And it is recommended to the legislature of this state, to provide by law against every corruption or partiality in the choice, return, or appointment of juries.

SECT. 26. Courts of sessions, common pleas, and orphans courts shall be held quarterly in each city and county; and the legislature shall have power to establish all such other courts as they may judge for the good of the inhabitants of the state. All courts shall be open, and justice shall be impartially administered without corruption or unnecessary delay: All their officers shall be paid an adequate but moderate compensation for their services: And if any officer shall take greater or other fees than the law allows him, either directly or indirectly, it shall ever after disqualify him from holding any office in this state.

SECT. 27. All prosecutions shall commence in the name and by the authority of the freemen of the commonwealth of Pennsylvania; and all indictments shall conclude with these words, "Against the peace and dignity of the same." The style of all process hereafter in this state shall be, The commonwealth of Pennsylvania.

SECT. 28. The person of a debtor, where there is not a strong presumption of fraud, shall not be continued in prison, after delivering Up, bona fide, all his estate real and personal, for the use of his creditors, in such manner as shall be hereafter regulated by law. All prisoners shall be bailable by sufficient sureties, unless for capital offences, when the proof is evident, or presumption great.

SECT. 29. Excessive bail shall not be exacted for bailable offences: And all fines shall be moderate.

SECT. 30. Justices of the peace shall be elected by the freeholders of each city and county respectively, that is to say, two or more persons may be chosen for each ward, township, or district, as the law shall hereafter direct: And their names shall be returned to the president in council, who shall commissionate one or more of them for each ward, township, or district so returning, for seven years, removable for misconduct by the general assembly. But if any city or county, ward, township, or district in this commonwealth, shall hereafter incline to change the manner of appointing their justices of the peace as settled in this article, the general assembly may make laws to regulate the same, agreeable to the desire of a majority of the freeholders of the city or county, ward, township, or district so applying. No justice of the peace shall sit in the general assembly unless he first resigns his commission; nor shall he be allowed to take any fees, nor any salary or allowance, except such as the future legislature may grant.

SECT. 31. Sheriffs and coroners shall be elected annually in each city and county, by the freemen; that is to say, two persons for each office, one of whom for each, is to be commissioned by the President in council. No person shall continue in the office of sheriff more than three successive years, or be capable of being again elected during four years afterwards. The election shall be held at the same time and place appointed for the election of representatives: And the commissioners and assessors, and other officers chosen by the people, shall also be then and there elected, as has been usual heretofore, until altered or otherwise regulated by the future legislature of this state.

SECT. 32. All elections, whether by the people or in general assembly, shall be by ballot, free and voluntary: And any elector, who shall receive any gift or reward for his vote, in meat, drink, monies, or otherwise, shall forfeit his right to elect for that time, and suffer such other penalties as future laws shall direct. And any person who shall directly or indirectly give, promise, or bestow any such rewards to be elected, shall be thereby rendered incapable to serve for the ensuing year.

SECT. 33. All fees, licence money, fines and forfeitures heretofore granted, or paid to the governor, or his deputies for the support of government, shall hereafter be paid into the public treasury, unless altered or abolished by the future legislature.

SECT. 34. A register's office for the probate of wills and granting letters of administration, and an office for the recording of deeds, shall be kept in each city and county: The officers to be appointed by the general assembly, removable at their pleasure, and to be commissioned by the president in council.

SECT. 35. The printing presses shall be free to every person who undertakes to examine the proceedings of the legislature, or any part of government.

SECT. 36. As every freeman to preserve his independence, (if without a sufficient estate) ought to have some profession, calling, trade or farm, whereby he may honestly subsist, there can be no necessity for, nor use in establishing offices of profit, the usual effects of which are dependence and servility unbecoming freemen, in the possessors and expectants; faction, contention, corruption, and disorder among the people. But if any man is called into public service; to the prejudice of his private affairs, he has a right to a reasonable compensation: And whenever an office, through increase of fees or otherwise, becomes so profitable as to occasion many to apply for it, the profits ought to be lessened by the legislature.

SECT. 37. The future legislature of this state, shall regulate intails in such a manner as to prevent perpetuities.

SECT. 38. The penal laws as heretofore used shall be reformed by the legislature of this state, as soon as may be, and punishments made in some cases less sanguinary, and in general more proportionate to the crimes.

SECT. 39. To deter more effectually from the commission of crimes by continued visible punishments of long duration, and to make sanguinary punishments less necessary; houses ought to be provided for punishing by hard labour, those who shall be convicted of crimes not capital; wherein the criminals shall be imployed for the benefit of the public, or for reparation of injuries done to private persons: And all persons at proper times shall be admitted to see the prisoners at their labour.

SECT. 40. Every officer, whether judicial, executive or military, in authority under this commonwealth, shall take the following oath or affirmation of allegiance, and general oath of office before he enters on the execution of his office.

THE OATH OR AFFIRMATION OF ALLEGIANCE

I _____ do swear (or affirm) that I will be true and faithful to the commonwealth of Pennsylvania: And that I will not directly or indirectly do any act or thing prejudicial or injurious to the constitution or government thereof, as established by the-convention.

THE OATH OR AFFIRMATION OF OFFICE

I _____ do swear (or affirm) that I will faithfully execute the office of _____ for the _____ of _____ and will do equal right and justice to all men, to the best of my judgment and abilities, according to law.

SECT. 41. No public tax, custom or contribution shall be imposed upon, or paid by the people of this state, except by a law for that purpose: And before any law be made for raising it, the purpose for which any tax is to be raised ought to appear clearly to the legislature to be of more service to the community than the money would be, if not collected; which being well observed, taxes can never be burthens.

SECT. 42. Every foreigner of good character who comes to settle in this state, having first taken an oath or affirmation of allegiance to the same, may purchase, or by other just means acquire, hold, and transfer land or other real estate; and after one year's residence, shall be deemed a free denizen thereof, and entitled to all the rights of a natural born subject of this state, except that he shall not be capable of being elected a representative until after two years residence.

SECT. 43. The inhabitants of this state shall have liberty to fowl and hunt in seasonable times on the lands they hold, and on all other lands therein not inclosed; and in like manner to fish in all boatable waters, and others not private property

SECT. 44. A school or schools shall be established in each county by the legislature, for the convenient instruction of youth, with such salaries to the masters paid by the public, as may enable them to instruct youth at low prices: And all useful learning shall be duly encouraged and promoted In one or more universities.

SECT. 45. Laws for the encouragement of virtue, and prevention of vice and immorality, shall be made and constantly kept in force, and provision shall be made for their due execution: And all religious societies or bodies of men heretofore united or incorporated for the advancement of religion or learning, or for other pious and charitable purposes, shall be encouraged and protected in the enjoyment of the privileges, immunities and estates which they were accustomed to enjoy, or could of right have enjoyed, under the laws and former constitution of this state.

SECT. 46. The declaration of rights is hereby declared to be a part of the constitution of this commonwealth, and ought never to be violated on any presence whatever.

SECT. 47. In order that the freedom of the commonwealth may be preserved inviolate forever, there shall be chosen by ballot by the freemen in each city and county respectively, on the second Tuesday in October, in the Year one thousand seven hundred and eighty-three, and on the second Tuesday in October, in every seventh year thereafter, two persons in each city and county of this state, to be called the COUNCIL OF CENSORS; who shall meet together on the second Monday of November next ensuing their election; the majority of whom shall be a quorum in every case, except as to calling a convention, in which two-thirds of the whole number elected shall agree: And whose duty it shall be to enquire whether the constitution has been preserved inviolate in every part; and whether the legislative and executive branches of government have performed their duty as guardians of the people, or assumed to themselves, or exercised other or greater powers than they are intitled to by the constitution: They are also to enquire whether the public taxes have been justly laid and collected in all parts of this commonwealth, in what manner the public monies have been disposed of, and whether the laws have been duly executed. For these purposes they shall have power to send for persons, papers, and records; they shall have authority to pass public censures, to order impeachments, and to recommend to the legislature the repealing such laws as appear to them to have been enacted contrary to the principles of the constitution. These powers they shall continue to have, for and during the space of one year from the day of their election and no longer: The said council of censors shall also have power to call a convention, to meet within two years

after their sitting, if there appear to them an absolute necessity of amending any article of the constitution which may be defective, explaining such as may be thought not clearly expressed, and of adding such as are necessary for the preservation of the rights and happiness of the people: But the articles to be amended, and the amendments proposed, and such articles as are proposed to be added or abolished, shall be promulgated at least six months before the day appointed for the election of such convention, for the previous consideration of the people, that they may have an opportunity of instructing their delegates on the subject.

DRAWING CONCLUSIONS:

1. In what ways, if any, were the state constitutions of Virginia and Pennsylvania more democratic than the US Constitution as drafted in 1787?
2. In what ways, if any, were the state constitutions of Virginia and Pennsylvania less democratic than the US Constitution as drafted in 1787?

1.5 THE BILL OF RIGHTS (1789)

Many opponents of the Constitution highlighted the absence of a bill of rights as a reason to reject the document. In response, supporters of the Constitution agreed that if the Constitution were ratified, they would immediately begin the amendment process to add a set of provisions to protect the rights of individuals from abuses by the federal government. The new Congress approved a set of proposed amendments during its initial session; and within two years, a sufficient number of states had ratified the ten amendments that became the Bill of Rights.

The Bill of Rights, with its focus on individual rights, is often considered the most egalitarian portion of the constitution. The failure to include a Bill of Rights in the Constitution as originally proposed can be cited as evidence of the anti-democratic tendencies of the Federalists. On the other hand, the quick addition of a Bill of Rights can be cited as evidence of the egalitarian sentiments that Federalists and anti-Federalists shared. Of course, the question remains—did the Bill of Rights actually protect the rights of everyone? As you read it, note that the Bill of Rights takes the form of a list of things that the federal government is not allowed to do as opposed to a list of rights that all individuals have.

GUIDING QUESTIONS:

1. What specific limits on the power of the federal government are included in the Bill of Rights? In other words, according to the Bill of Rights, what can't the federal government do?

THE BILL OF RIGHTS

Congress of the United States begun and held at the City of New-York, on Wednesday the fourth of March, one thousand seven hundred and eighty nine.

THE Conventions of a number of the States, having at the time of their adopting the Constitution, expressed a desire, in order to prevent misconstruction or abuse of its powers, that further declaratory and restrictive clauses should be added: And as extending the ground of public confidence in the Government, will best ensure the beneficent ends of its institution.

RESOLVED by the Senate and House of Representatives of the United States of America, in Congress assembled, two thirds of both Houses concurring, that the following Articles be proposed to the Legislatures of the several States, as amendments to the Constitution of the United States, all, or any of which Articles, when ratified by three fourths of the said Legislatures, to be valid to all intents and purposes, as part of the said Constitution; viz.

ARTICLES in addition to, and Amendment of the Constitution of the United States of America, proposed by Congress, and ratified by the Legislatures of the several States, pursuant to the fifth Article of the original Constitution.

AMENDMENT I

Congress shall make no law respecting an establishment of religion, or prohibiting the free exercise thereof; or abridging the freedom of speech, or of the press; or the right of the people peaceably to assemble, and to petition the Government for a redress of grievances.

The Bill of Rights: A Transcription, National Archives and Records Administration https://www.archives.gov/founding-docs/bill-of-rights-transcript

AMENDMENT II

A well regulated Militia, being necessary to the security of a free State, the right of the people to keep and bear Arms, shall not be infringed.

AMENDMENT III

No Soldier shall, in time of peace be quartered in any house, without the consent of the Owner, nor in time of war, but in a manner to be prescribed by law.

AMENDMENT IV

The right of the people to be secure in their persons, houses, papers, and effects, against unreasonable searches and seizures, shall not be violated, and no Warrants shall issue, but upon probable cause, supported by Oath or affirmation, and particularly describing the place to be searched, and the persons or things to be seized.

AMENDMENT V

No person shall be held to answer for a capital, or otherwise infamous crime, unless on a presentment or indictment of a Grand Jury, except in cases arising in the land or naval forces, or in the Militia, when in actual service in time of War or public danger; nor shall any person be subject for the same offence to be twice put in jeopardy of life or limb; nor shall be compelled in any criminal case to be a witness against himself, nor be deprived of life, liberty, or property, without due process of law; nor shall private property be taken for public use, without just compensation.

AMENDMENT VI

In all criminal prosecutions, the accused shall enjoy the right to a speedy and public trial, by an impartial jury of the State and district wherein the crime shall have been committed, which district shall have been previously ascertained by law, and to be informed of the nature and cause of the accusation; to be confronted with the witnesses against him; to have compulsory process for obtaining witnesses in his favor, and to have the Assistance of Counsel for his defence.

AMENDMENT VII

In Suits at common law, where the value in controversy shall exceed twenty dollars, the right of trial by jury shall be preserved, and no fact tried by a jury, shall be otherwise re-examined in any Court of the United States, than according to the rules of the common law.

AMENDMENT VIII

Excessive bail shall not be required, nor excessive fines imposed, nor cruel and unusual punishments inflicted.

AMENDMENT IX

The enumeration in the Constitution, of certain rights, shall not be construed to deny or disparage others retained by the people.

AMENDMENT X

The powers not delegated to the United States by the Constitution, nor prohibited by it to the States, are reserved to the States respectively, or to the people.

DRAWING CONCLUSIONS:

1. What are the most important individual rights protected by the Bill of Rights?
2. What rights (or whose rights) did the Bill of Rights not protect?

FEDERALIST DOCUMENTS

Examining the writings of the architects of the Constitution is one of the most effective ways to determine their goals and motives. The documents that follow were written by Alexander Hamilton and James Madison, the two most influential of the Constitutional architects. Some of these documents were private, while others were intended for a public audience. As you examine each source, pay close attention to the context in which it was written. Take into consideration the author's motive for creating each separate piece of writing, as well as the his intended audience.

2.1 LETTER FROM ALEXANDER HAMILTON TO JAMES DUANE (1780)

Alexander Hamilton was an early critic of the operations of the federal Congress, which prior to the ratification of the Articles of Confederation in 1781 acted without any clear rules or guidelines whatsoever. In this 1780 letter to prominent New York political leader James Duane, Hamilton offers both a critique of the existing Congress and of the proposed Articles of Confederation. At the time of this letter, the Revolutionary War was still underway, and victory was far from certain. Hamilton raises the issue of whether the existing Congress had the capacity to successfully wage the war and to govern the nation in the hoped for postwar peace.

GUIDING QUESTIONS:

1. What specific concerns does Hamilton raise regarding the operations of the existing Congress?
2. What specific criticisms does he make of the proposed Articles of Confederation?
3. What are some of the specific suggestions he makes for restructuring the federal government?

ALEXANDER HAMILTON TO JAMES DUANE

LIBERTY POLE, September 3, 1780.

DEAR SIR:

Agreeably to your request, and my promise, I sit down to give you my ideas of the defects of our present system, and the changes necessary to save us from ruin. They may perhaps be the reveries of a projector rather than the sober views of a politician. You will judge of them, and make what use you please of them.

The fundamental defect is a want of power in Congress. It is hardly worth while to show in what this consists, as it seems to be universally acknowledged, or to point out how it has happened, as the only question is how to remedy it. It may however be said that it has originated from three causes—an excess of the spirit of liberty which has made the particular states show a jealousy of all power not in their own hands—and this jealousy has led them to exercise a right of judging in the last resort of the measures recommended by Congress, and of acting according to their own opinions of their propriety or necessity, a diffidence in Congress of their own powers, by which they have been timid and indecisive in their resolutions, constantly making concessions to the states, till they have scarcely left themselves the shadow of power; a want of sufficient means at their disposal to answer the public exigencies and of vigor to draw forth those means; which have occasioned them to depend on the states individually to fulfil their engagements with the army,—and the consequence of which has been to ruin their influence and credit with the army, to establish its dependence on each state separately rather than *on them*,—that is, rather than on the whole collectively.

It may be pleaded, that Congress had never any definitive powers granted them and of course could exercise none—could do nothing more than recommend. The manner in which Congress was appointed would warrant, and the public good required, that they should have considered themselves as vested with full power *to preserve the republic from harm.* They have done many of the highest acts of sovereignty, which were always cheerfully submitted to: the declaration of independence, the declaration of

From Henry Cabot Lodge, ed., *The Works of Alexander Hamilton*, vol. 1 (New York: G.P. Putnam's Sons, 1904), 213–222.

war, the levying [of] an army, creating a navy, emitting money, making alliances with foreign powers, appointing a dictator, etc. All these implications of a complete sovereignty were never disputed, and ought to have been a standard for the whole conduct of Administration. Undefined powers are discretionary powers, limited only by the object for which they were given; in the present case, the independence and freedom of America. The confederation made no difference; for as it has not been generally adopted, it had no operation. But from what I recollect of it, Congress have even descended from the authority which the spirit of that act gives them, while the particular states have no further attended to it than as it suited their pretensions and convenience. It would take too much time to enter into particular instances, each of which separately might appear inconsiderable; but united are of serious import. I only mean to remark, not to censure.

But the confederation itself is defective and requires to be altered; it is neither fit for war, nor peace. The idea of an uncontrollable sovereignty in each state, over its internal police, will defeat the other powers given to Congress, and make our union feeble and precarious. There are instances without number, where acts necessary for the general good, and which rise out of the powers given to Congress must interfere with the internal police of the states, and there are as many instances in which the particular states by arrangements of internal police can effectually though indirectly counteract the arrangements of Congress. You have already had examples of this for which I refer you to your own memory.

The confederation gives the states individually too much influence in the affairs of the army; they should have nothing to do with it. The entire formation and disposal of our military forces ought to belong to Congress. It is an essential cement of the union; and it ought to be the policy of Congress to destroy all ideas of state attachments in the army and make it look up wholly to them. For this purpose all appointments promotions and provisions whatsoever ought to be made by them. It may be apprehended that this may be dangerous to liberty. But nothing appears more evident to me, than that we run much greater risk of having a weak and disunited federal government, than one which will be able to usurp upon the rights of the people.

Already some of the lines of the army would obey their states in opposition to Congress notwithstanding the pains we have taken to preserve the unity of the army. If any thing would hinder this it would be the personal influence of the General—a melancholy and mortifying consideration.

The forms of our state constitutions must always give them great weight in our affairs and will make it too difficult to bend them to the pursuit of a common interest, too easy to oppose whatever they do not like and to form partial combinations subversive of the general one. There is a wide difference between our situation and that of an empire under one simple form of government, distributed into counties provinces or districts, which have no Legislatures but merely magistratical bodies to execute the laws of a common sovereign. Here the danger is that the sovereign will have too much power to oppress the parts of which it is composed. In our case, that of an empire composed of confederated states each with a government completely organized within itself, having all the means to draw its subjects to a close dependence on itself—the danger is directly the reverse. It is that the common sovereign will not have power sufficient to unite the different members together, and direct the common forces to the interest and happiness of the whole.

The leagues among the old Grecian republics are a proof of this. They were continually at war with each other, and for want of union fell a prey to their neighbors. They frequently held general councils, but their resolutions were no further observed than as they suited the interests and inclinations of all the parties and at length, they sunk entirely into contempt.

The Swiss Cantons are another proof of the doctrine. They have had wars with each other which would have been fatal to them, had not the different powers in their neighborhood been too jealous of one-another and too equally matched to suffer either to take advantage of their quarrels. That they have remained so long united at all is to be attributed to their weakness, to their poverty, and to the cause just mentioned. These ties will not exist in America; a little time hence, some of the states will be powerful empires, and we are so remote from other nations that we shall have all the leisure and opportunity we can wish to cut each other's throats.

The Germanic corps might also be cited as an example in favor of the position.

The United provinces may be thought to be one against it. But the family of the Stadtholders, whose authority is interwoven with the whole government, has been a strong link of union between them. Their physical necessities and the habits founded upon them have contributed to it. Each province is too inconsiderable, by itself, to undertake any thing. An analysis of their present constitutions would show that they have many ties which would not exist in ours; and that they are by no means a proper mode for us.

Our own experience should satisfy us. We have felt the difficulty of drawing out the resources of the country and inducing the states to combine in equal exertions for the common cause. The ill success of our last attempt is striking. Some have done a great deal, others little or scarcely any thing. The disputes about boundaries, etc., testify how flattering a prospect we have of future tranquility, if we do not frame in time a confederacy capable of deciding the differences and compelling the obedience of the respective members.

The Confederation, too, gives the power of the purse too entirely to the state legislatures. It should provide perpetual funds in the disposal of Congress, by a land tax, poll tax, or the like. All imposts upon commerce ought to be laid by Congress and appropriated to their use, for without certain revenues, a government can have no power; that power, which holds the purse–strings absolutely, must rule. This seems to be a medium which, without making Congress altogether independent, will tend to give reality to its authority.

Another defect in our system is want of method and energy in the administration. This has partly resulted from the other defect; but in a great degree from prejudice and the want of a proper executive. Congress have kept the power too much into their own hands and have meddled too much with details of every sort. Congress is, properly, a deliberative corps, and it forgets itself when it attempts to play the executive. It is impossible such a body, numerous as it is, constantly fluctuating, can ever act with sufficient decision, or with system. Two thirds of the members, one half the time, cannot know what has gone before them or what connection the subject in hand has to what has been transacted on former occasions. The members, who have been more permanent, will only give information, that promotes the side they espouse, in the present case, and will as often mislead as enlighten. The variety of business must distract, and the proneness of every assembly to debate must at all times delay.

Lately, Congress, convinced of these inconveniences, have gone into the measure of appointing boards. But this is in my opinion a bad plan.

A single man, in each department of the administration, would be greatly preferable. It would give us a chance of more knowledge, more activity, more responsibility, and, of course, more zeal and attention. Boards partake of a part of the inconveniencies of larger assemblies. Their decisions are slower their energy less their responsibility more diffused. They will not have the same abilities and knowledge as an administration by single men. Men of the first pretensions will not so readily engage in them, because they will be less conspicuous, of less importance, have less opportunity of distinguishing themselves. The members of boards will take less pains to inform themselves and arrive to eminence, because they have fewer motives to do it. All these reasons conspire to give a preference to the plan of vesting the great executive departments of the state in the hands of individuals. As these men will be, of course, at all times under the direction of Congress, we shall blend the advantages of a monarchy and republic in our constitution.

A question has been made, whether single men could be found to undertake these offices. I think they could, because there would be then every thing to excite the ambition of candidates. But, in order to effect this, Congress, by their manner of appointing them and the line of duty marked out, must show that they are in earnest in making these offices, offices of real trust and importance.

I fear a little vanity has stood in the way of these arrangements, as though they would lessen the importance of Congress and leave them nothing to do.

But they would have precisely the same rights and powers as heretofore, happily disencumbered of the detail. They would have to inspect the conduct of their ministers, deliberate upon their plans, originate others for the public good; only observing this rule— that they ought to consult their ministers, and get all the information and advice they could from them, before they entered into any new measures or made changes in the old.

A third defect is the fluctuating constitution of our army. This has been a pregnant source of evil; all our military misfortunes, three fourths of our civil embarrassments are to be ascribed to it. The General has so fully enumerated the mischiefs of it, in a late letter of 20 August 1780, to Congress, that I could only repeat what he has said, and will therefore refer you to that letter.

The imperfect and unequal provision made for the army is a fourth defect, which you will find delineated in the same letter. Without a speedy change the army must dissolve. It is now a mob, rather than an army, without clothing, without pay, without provision, without morals, without discipline. We begin to hate the country for its neglect of us; the country begins to hate us for our oppressions of them. Congress have long been jealous of us; we have now lost all confidence in them, and give the worst construction to all they do. Held together by the slenderest ties we are ripening for a dissolution.

The present mode of supplying the army, by state purchases, is not one of the least considerable defects of our system. It is too precarious a dependence, because the states will never be sufficiently impressed with our necessities. Each will make its own ease a primary object, the supply of the army a secondary one. The variety of channels through which the business is transacted will multiply the number of persons employed and the opportunities of embezzling public money. From the popular spirit on which most of the governments turn, the state agents, will be men of less character and ability, nor will there be so rigid a responsibility among them as there might easily be among those in the employ of the Continent; of course not so much diligence care or economy. Very little of the money raised in the several states will go into the Continental treasury, on pretence that it is all exhausted in providing the quotas of supplies, and the public will be without funds for the other demands of governments. The expense will be ultimately much greater and the advantages much smaller. We actually feel the insufficiency of this plan, and have reason to dread under it a ruinous extremity of want.

These are the principal defects in the present system that now occur to me. There are many inferior ones in the organization of particular departments and many errors of administration, which might be pointed out, but the task would be troublesome and tedious; and if we had once remedied those I have mentioned, the others would not be attended with much difficulty.

DRAWING CONCLUSION:

1. What do the criticisms that Hamilton makes and suggestions that he offers reveal about his motives and his long-term goals and objectives?

2.2 ALEXANDER HAMILTON, "CONJECTURES ABOUT THE CONSTITUTION" (1787)

Alexander Hamilton wrote this essay in September 1787 shortly after the Constitutional Convention completed its work. The essay was never published, and it is unclear the purpose for which Hamilton wrote it. In the essay, Hamilton analyzes the prospects for a successful ratification of the proposed document. He identifies likely supporters and likely opponents of the proposed constitution and reflects on the motivations of both groups. As you read, note that Hamilton paints the motivations of Federalists in a much more positive light than anti-Federalists.

GUIDING QUESTIONS:

1. What groups does Hamilton say will likely support the proposed constitution? What does he say their motives are?
2. What groups does Hamilton say will likely oppose the proposed constitution? What does he say their motives are?

CONJECTURES ABOUT THE NEW CONSTITUTION

[september 17–30, 1787]

The new constitution has in favour of its success these circumstances—a very great weight of influence of the persons who framed it, particularly in the universal popularity of General Washington—the good will of the commercial interest throughout the states which will give all its efforts to the establishment of a government capable of regulating protecting and extending the commerce of the Union—the good will of most men of property in the several states who wish a government of the union able to protect them against domestic violence and the depredations which the democratic spirit is apt to make on property; and who are besides anxious for the respectability of the nation—the hopes of the Creditors of the United States that a general government possessing the means of doing it will pay the debt of the Union—a strong belief in the people at large of the insufficiency of the present confederation to preserve the existence of the Union and of the necessity of the union to their safety and prosperity; of course a strong desire of a change and a predisposition to receive well the propositions of the Convention.

Against its success is to be put the dissent of two or three important men in the Convention; who will think their characters pleged to defeat the plan—the influence of many *inconsiderable* men in possession of considerable offices under the state governments who will fear a diminution of their consequence, power and emolument by the establishment of the general government and who can hope for nothing there—the influence of some *considerable* men in office possessed of talents and popularity who partly from the same motives and partly from a desire of *playing a part* in a convulsion for their own aggrandisement will oppose the quiet adoption of the new government—(some considerable men out of office, from motives of <am>bition may be disposed to act the same part)—add <to> these causes the disinclination of the people to taxes, and of course to a strong government—the opposition of all men much in debt who will not wish to see a government established one object of which

From Harold S. Syrett, ed., *The Papers of Alexander Hamilton*, vol. 4 (New York: Columbia University Press, 1962), 275–277.

is to restrain the means of cheating Creditors—the democratical jealousy of the people which may be alarmed at the appearance of institutions that may seem calculated to place the power of the community in few hands and to raise a few individuals to stations of great preeminence—and the influence of some foreign powers who from different motives will not wish to see an energetic government established throughout the states.

In this view of the subject it is difficult to form any judgment whether the plan will be adopted or rejected. It must be essentially [a] matter of conjecture. The present appearances and all other circumstances considered the probability seems to be on the side of its adoption.

But the causes operating against its adoption are powerful and there will be nothing astonishing in the Contrary.

If it do not finally obtain, it is probable the discussion of the question will beget such struggles animosities and heats in the community that this circumstance conspiring with the *real necessity* of an essential change in our present situation will produce civil war. Should this happen, whatever parties prevail it is probable governments very different from the present in their principles will be established. A dismemberment of the Union and monarchies in different portions of it may be expected. It may however happen that no civil war will take place; but several republican confederacies be established between different combinations of the particular states.

A reunion with Great Britain, from universal disgust at a state of commotion, is not impossible, though not much to be feared. The most plausible shape of such a business would be the establishment of a son of the present monarch in the supreme government of this country with a family compact.

If the government be adopted, it is probable general Washington will be the President of the United States. This will insure a wise choice of men to administer the government and a good administration. A good administration will conciliate the confidence and affection of the people and perhaps enable the government to acquire more consistency than the proposed constitution seems to promise for so great a Country. It may then triumph altogether over the state governments and reduce them to an intire subordination, dividing the larger states into smaller districts. The *organs* of the general government may also acquire additional strength.

If this should not be the case, in the course of a few years, it is probable that the contests about the boundaries of power between the particular governments and the general government and the *momentum* of the larger states in such contests will produce a dissolution of the Union. This after all seems to be the most likely result.

But it is almost arrogance in so complicated a subject, depending so intirely on the incalculable fluctuations of the human passions, to attempt even a conjecture about the event.

It will be Eight or Nine months before any certain judgment can be formed respecting the adoption of the Plan.

DRAWING CONCLUSION:

1. What does Hamilton's analysis of the forces arrayed for and against the proposed constitution reveal about his own motives and political goals?

2.3   JAMES MADISON, "VICES OF THE POLITICAL SYSTEM OF THE UNITED STATES" (1787)

In April 1787, shortly before the Constitutional Convention began meeting, James Madison composed the following private memo in which he summarized what he considered to be the main defects of the Articles of Confederation. Madison most likely wrote this memo to gather and clarify his own thoughts in preparation for the convention. The document lists twelve defects of the Articles and elaborates on each one. Note that the phrase "want of" in the list of defects simply means "lack of." You may want to pay particular attention to Section 11.

GUIDING QUESTIONS:

1. What does Madison consider to be defects with the system of government established by the Articles of Confederation?
2. Of the defects he lists, which ones seem most significant? Which ones are most revealing of Madison's motives and his broader goals and objectives?

VICES OF THE POLITICAL SYSTEM OF THE U. STATES

Observations by J.M. (a copy taken by permission by Danl. Carroll & sent to Chs Carroll of Carrollton)

1. Failure of the States to comply with the Constitutional requisitions.

1. This evil has been so fully experienced both during the war and since the peace, results so naturally from the number and independent authority of the States and has been so uniformly exemplified in every similar Confederacy, that it may be considered as not less radically and permanently inherent in, than it is fatal to the object of, the present System.

2. Encroachments by the States on the federal authority.

2. Examples of this are numerous and repetitions may be foreseen in almost every case where any favorite object of a State shall present a temptation. Among these examples are the wars and Treaties of Georgia with the Indians—The unlicensed compacts between Virginia and Maryland, and between Pena.

[Pennsylvania] & N. Jersey—the troops raised and to be kept up by Massts. [Massachusetts]

3. Violations of the law of nations and of treaties.

3. From the number of Legislatures, the sphere of life from which most of their members are taken, and the circumstances under which their legislative business is carried on, irregularities of this kind must frequently happen. Accordingly not a year has passed without instances of them in some one or other of the States. The Treaty of peace—the treaty with France—the treaty with Holland have each been violated. [See the complaints to Congress on these subjects.] The causes of these irregularities must necessarily produce frequent violations of the law of nations in other respects.

As yet foreign powers have not been rigorous in animadverting on us. This moderation however cannot be mistaken for a permanent partiality to our faults, or a permanent security agst. those disputes with other nations, which being among the greatest of public calamities, it ought to be least in the power of any part of the Community to bring on the whole.

From Robert A. Rutland, ed., *The Papers of James Madison*, vol. 9 (Chicago: University of Chicago Press, 1975), 348–357.

4. Trespasses of the States on the rights of each other.

4. These are alarming symptoms, and may be daily apprehended as we are admonished by daily experience. See the law of Virginia restricting foreign vessels to certain ports—of Maryland in favor of vessels belonging to her own citizens—of N. York in favor of the same.

Paper money, instalments of debts, occlusion of Courts, making property a legal tender, may likewise be deemed aggressions on the rights of other States. As the Citizens of every State aggregately taken stand more or less in the relation of Creditors or debtors, to the Citizens of every other States, Acts of the debtor State in favor of debtors, affect the Creditor State, in the same manner, as they do its own citizens who are relatively creditors towards other citizens. This remark may be extended to foreign nations. If the exclusive regulation of the value and alloy of coin was properly delegated to the federal authority, the policy of it equally requires a controul on the States in the cases above mentioned. It must have been meant 1. to preserve uniformity in the circulating medium throughout the nation. 2. to prevent those frauds on the citizens of other States, and the subjects of foreign powers, which might disturb the tranquility at home, or involve the Union in foreign contests.

The practice of many States in restricting the commercial intercourse with other States, and putting their productions and manufactures on the same footing with those of foreign nations, though not contrary to the federal articles, is certainly adverse to the spirit of the Union, and tends to beget retaliating regulations, not less expensive & vexatious in themselves, than they are destructive of the general harmony.

5. want of concert in matters where common interest requires it.

5. This defect is strongly illustrated in the state of our commercial affairs. How much has the national dignity, interest, and revenue suffered from this cause? Instances of inferior moment are the want of uniformity in the laws concerning naturalization & literary property; of provision for national seminaries, for grants of incorporation for national purposes, for canals and other works of general utility, wch. may at present be defeated by the perverseness of particular States whose concurrence is necessary.

6. want of guaranty to the States of their Constitutions & laws against internal violence.

6. The confederation is silent on this point and therefore by the second article the hands of the federal authority are tied. According to Republican Theory, Right and power being both vested in the majority, are held to be synonimous. According to fact and experience a minority may in an appeal to force, be an overmatch for the majority. 1. If the minority happen to include all such as possess the skill and habits of military life, & such as possess the great pecuniary resources, one third only may conquer the remaining two thirds. 2. One third of those who participate in the choice of the rulers, may be rendered a majority by the accession of those whose poverty excludes them from a right of suffrage, and who for obvious reasons will be more likely to join the standard of sedition than that of the established Government. 3. Where slavery exists the republican Theory becomes still more fallacious.

. . .

11. Injustice of the laws of States.

11. If the multiplicity and mutability of laws prove a want of wisdom, their injustice betrays a defect still more alarming: more alarming not merely because it is a greater evil in itself, but because it brings more into question the fundamental principle of republican Government, that the majority who rule in such Governments, are the safest Guardians both of public Good and of private rights. To what causes is this evil to be ascribed?

These causes lie: 1. in the Representative bodies.
2. in the people themselves.

1. Representative appointments are sought from 3 motives. 1. ambition 2. personal interest. 3. public good. Unhappily the two first are proved by experience to be most prevalent. Hence the candidates who feel them, particularly, the second, are most industrious, and most successful in pursuing their object: and forming often a majority in the legislative Councils, with interested views, contrary to the interest, and views, of their Constituents, join in a perfidious

sacrifice of the latter to the former. A succeeding election it might be supposed, would displace the offenders, and repair the mischief. But how easily are base and selfish measures, masked by pretexts of public good and apparent expediency? How frequently will a repetition of the same arts and industry which succeeded in the first instance, again prevail on the unwary to misplace their confidence?

How frequently too will the honest but unenlightened representative be the dupe of a favorite leader, veiling his selfish views under the professions of public good, and varnishing his sophistical arguments with the glowing colours of popular eloquence?

2. A still more fatal if not more frequent cause lies among the people themselves. All civilized societies are divided into different interests and factions, as they happen to be creditors or debtors—Rich or poor—husbandmen, merchants or manufacturers—members of different religious sects—followers of different political leaders—inhabitants of different districts—owners of different kinds of property &c &c. In republican Government the majority however composed, ultimately give the law. Whenever therefore an apparent interest or common passion unites a majority what is to restrain them from unjust violations of the rights and interests of the minority, or of individuals? Three motives only 1. a prudent regard to their own good as involved in the general and permanent good of the Community. This consideration although of decisive weight in itself, is found by experience to be too often unheeded. It is too often forgotten, by nations as well as by individuals that honesty is the best policy. 2dly. respect for character. However strong this motive may be in individuals, it is considered as very insufficient to restrain them from injustice. In a multitude its efficacy is diminished in proportion to the number which is to share the praise or the blame. Besides, as it has reference to public opinion, which within a particular Society, is the opinion of the majority, the standard is fixed by those whose conduct is to be measured by it. The public opinion without the Society, will be little respected by the people at large of any Country. Individuals of extended views, and of national pride, may bring the public proceedings to this standard, but the

example will never be followed by the multitude. Is it to be imagined that an ordinary citizen or even an assemblyman of R. Island in estimating the policy of paper money, ever considered or cared in what light the measure would be viewed in France or Holland; or even in Massts or Connect.? It was a sufficient temptation to both that it was for their interest: it was a sufficient sanction to the latter that it was popular in the State; to the former that it was so in the neighbourhood. 3dly. will Religion the only remaining motive be a sufficient restraint? It is not pretended to be such on men individually considered. Will its effect be greater on them considered in an aggregate view? quite the reverse. The conduct of every popular assembly acting on oath, the strongest of religious Ties, proves that individuals join without remorse in acts, against which their consciences would revolt if proposed to them under the like sanction, separately in their closets. When indeed Religion is kindled into enthusiasm, its force like that of other passions, is increased by the sympathy of a multitude. But enthusiasm is only a temporary state of religion, and while it lasts will hardly be seen with pleasure at the helm of Government. Besides as religion in its coolest state, is not infallible, it may become a motive to oppression as well as a restraint from injustice. Place three individuals in a situation wherein the interest of each depends on the voice of the others, and give to two of them an interest opposed to the rights of the third? Will the latter be secure? The prudence of every man would shun the danger. The rules & forms of justice suppose & guard against it. Will two thousand in a like situation be less likely to encroach on the rights of one thousand? The contrary is witnessed by the notorious factions & oppressions which take place in corporate towns limited as the opportunities are, and in little republics when uncontrouled by apprehensions of external danger. If an enlargement of the sphere is found to lessen the insecurity of private rights, it is not because the impulse of a common interest or passion is less predominant in this case with the majority; but because a common interest or passion is less apt to be felt and the requisite combinations less easy to be formed by a great than by a small number. The Society becomes broken into a greater variety of interests, of pursuits, of passions, which check each other, whilst those who may feel a common sentiment have less opportunity of communication and concert. It may be inferred that the inconveniences of popular States contrary to the prevailing Theory, are in proportion not to the extent, but to the narrowness of their limits.

The great desideratum in Government is such a modification of the Sovereignty as will render it sufficiently neutral between the different interests and factions, to controul one part of the Society from invading the rights of another, and at the same time sufficiently controuled itself, from setting up an interest adverse to that of the whole Society. In absolute Monarchies, the prince is sufficiently, neutral towards his subjects, but frequently sacrifices their happiness to his ambition or his avarice. In small Republics, the sovereign will is sufficiently controuled from such a Sacrifice of the entire Society, but is not sufficiently neutral towards the parts composing it. As a limited Monarchy tempers the evils of an absolute one; so an extensive Republic meliorates the administration of a small Republic.

An auxiliary desideratum for the melioration of the Republican form is such a process of elections as will most certainly extract from the mass of the Society the purest and noblest characters which it contains; such as will at once feel most strongly the proper motives to pursue the end of their appointment, and be most capable to devise the proper means of attaining it.

12. Impotence of the laws of the States

DRAWING CONCLUSION:

1. What does Madison's analysis of the defects of the Articles reveal about his political motives as well as his goals and objectives heading into the Constitutional Convention?

2.4 JAMES MADISON, "FEDERALIST NO. 10" (1787)

The most famous of the all the Federalist writings is a series of pro-ratification newspaper articles written by Alexander Hamilton, James Madison, and John Jay that came to be known as "The Federalist Papers." Originally appearing in New York newspapers between October 1787 and August 1788, and published anonymously under the pen name "Publius" (a Latin word meaning "of the people"), the Federalist Papers were intended to make the case for ratification of the proposed constitution, which was by no means a foregone conclusion. A total of eighty-five essays comprise the Federalist Papers. Two of the most famous articles (both authored by James Madison) are provided here.

Over time, many scholars came to view the Federalist Papers as the clearest and most comprehensive statement of the political thought of the founding fathers. As you read these, however, keep in mind that they were originally intended as *persuasive* documents that were designed to sway public opinion in favor of the proposed constitution.

One of the most powerful arguments of the anti-Federalists was that a shift in power from the state to the federal level would make government less responsive to the people. In Federalist No. 10, James Madison flips that argument on it head by asserting that republican forms of government (i.e., governments comprised of elected leaders) are actually more sustainable when they govern a larger territory. Among the greatest threats to a republic, Madison argues, are conflicts among what he calls "factions." By "faction" he means a group of people who are united around a common interest that is opposed to the rights of others and to the good of the community as a whole, what today is often called a "special interest group." Small republics can easily be disrupted by the "violence of faction," he claims, while larger republics are better able to withstand the disruptive influence of factions. A shift in power from the states to the federal government would, therefore, actually make the republic more secure. As you ponder Madison's argument, think about what it reveals about his overall political philosophy.

GUIDING QUESTIONS:

1. What does Madison say is the most common cause of the division of a community or nation into factions?
2. What does Madison consider to be the most dangerous type of faction? Why does he consider this particular type of faction so dangerous?
3. How, according to Madison, will the creation of a larger republic help to combat the evils of factions?

THE FEDERALIST NO. 10

THE UNION AS A SAFEGUARD AGAINST DOMESTIC FACTION AND INSURRECTION

JAMES MADISON

To the People of the State of New York:

AMONG the numerous advantages promised by a well-constructed Union, none deserves to be more accurately developed than its tendency to break and control the violence of faction. The friend of popular governments never finds himself so much alarmed for their character and fate, as when he contemplates their propensity to this dangerous vice. He will not fail, therefore, to set a due value on any plan which, without violating the principles to which he is attached, provides a proper cure for it. The instability, injustice, and confusion introduced into the public councils, have, in truth, been the mortal diseases under which popular governments have everywhere perished; as they continue to be the favorite and fruitful topics from which the adversaries to liberty derive their most specious declamations. The valuable improvements made by the American constitutions on the popular models, both ancient and modern, cannot certainly be too much admired; but it would be an unwarrantable partiality, to contend that they have as effectually obviated the danger on this side, as was wished and expected. Complaints are everywhere heard from our most considerate and virtuous citizens, equally the friends of public and private faith, and of public and personal liberty, that our governments are too unstable, that the public good is disregarded in the conflicts of rival parties, and that measures are too often decided, not according to the rules of justice and the rights of the minor party, but by the superior force of an interested and overbearing majority. However anxiously we may wish that these complaints had no foundation, the evidence, of known facts will not permit us to deny that they are in some degree true. It will be found, indeed, on a candid review of our situation, that some of the distresses under which we labor have been erroneously charged on the operation of our governments; but it will be found, at the same time, that other causes will not alone account for many of our heaviest misfortunes; and, particularly, for that prevailing and increasing distrust of public engagements, and alarm for private rights, which are echoed from one end of the continent to the other. These must be chiefly, if not wholly, effects of the unsteadiness and injustice with which a factious spirit has tainted our public administrations.

By a faction, I understand a number of citizens, whether amounting to a majority or a minority of the whole, who are united and actuated by some common impulse of passion, or of interest, adversed to the rights of other citizens, or to the permanent and aggregate interests of the community.

There are two methods of curing the mischiefs of faction: the one, by removing its causes; the other, by controlling its effects.

There are again two methods of removing the causes of faction: the one, by destroying the liberty which is essential to its existence; the other, by giving to every citizen the same opinions, the same passions, and the same interests.

It could never be more truly said than of the first remedy, that it was worse than the disease. Liberty is to faction what air is to fire, an aliment without which it instantly expires. But it could not be less folly to abolish liberty, which is essential to political life, because it nourishes faction, than it would be to wish the annihilation of air, which is essential to animal life, because it imparts to fire its destructive agency.

The second expedient is as impracticable as the first would be unwise. As long as the reason of man continues fallible, and he is at liberty to exercise it, different opinions will be formed. As long as the connection subsists between his reason and his self-love, his opinions and his passions will have a reciprocal influence on each other; and the former will be objects to which the latter will attach themselves. The diversity in the faculties of men, from which the rights of property originate, is not less an insuperable obstacle to a uniformity of interests. The protection of these faculties is the first object of government. From the protection of different and unequal faculties of acquiring property, the possession of different degrees and kinds of property immediately results; and from the influence of these on the sentiments and views of the respective proprietors, ensues a division of the society into different interests and parties.

The latent causes of faction are thus sown in the nature of man; and we see them everywhere brought into different degrees of activity, according to the different circumstances of civil society. A zeal for different opinions concerning religion, concerning government, and many other points, as well of speculation as of practice; an attachment to different leaders ambitiously contending for pre-eminence and power; or to persons of other descriptions whose fortunes have been interesting to the human passions, have, in turn, divided mankind into parties, inflamed them with mutual animosity, and rendered them much more disposed to vex and oppress each other than to co-operate for their common good. So strong is this propensity of mankind to fall into mutual animosities, that where no substantial occasion presents itself, the most frivolous and fanciful distinctions have been sufficient to kindle their unfriendly passions and excite their most violent conflicts. But the most common and durable source of factions has been the various and unequal distribution of property. Those who hold and those who are without property have ever formed distinct interests in society. Those who are creditors, and those who are debtors, fall under a like discrimination. A landed interest, a manufacturing interest, a mercantile interest, a moneyed interest, with many lesser interests, grow up of necessity in civilized nations, and divide them into different classes, actuated by different sentiments and views. The regulation of these various and interfering interests forms the principal task of modern legislation, and involves the spirit of party and faction in the necessary and ordinary operations of the government. . . .

The inference to which we are brought is, that the CAUSES of faction cannot be removed, and that relief is only to be sought in the means of controlling its EFFECTS.

If a faction consists of less than a majority, relief is supplied by the republican principle, which enables the majority to defeat its sinister views by regular vote. It may clog the administration, it may convulse the society; but it will be unable to execute and mask its violence under the forms of the Constitution. When a majority is included in a faction, the form of popular government, on the other hand, enables it to sacrifice to its ruling passion or interest both the public good and the rights of other citizens. To secure the public good and private rights against the danger of such a faction, and at the same time to preserve the spirit and the form of popular government, is then the great object to which our inquiries are directed. Let me add that it is the great desideratum by which this form of government can be rescued from the opprobrium under which it has so long labored, and be recommended to the esteem and adoption of mankind.

By what means is this object attainable? Evidently by one of two only. Either the existence of the same passion or interest in a majority at the same time must be prevented, or the majority, having such coexistent passion or interest, must be rendered, by their number and local situation, unable to concert and carry into effect schemes of oppression. If the impulse and the opportunity be suffered to coincide,

we well know that neither moral nor religious motives can be relied on as an adequate control. They are not found to be such on the injustice and violence of individuals, and lose their efficacy in proportion to the number combined together, that is, in proportion as their efficacy becomes needful.

From this view of the subject it may be concluded that a pure democracy, by which I mean a society consisting of a small number of citizens, who assemble and administer the government in person, can admit of no cure for the mischiefs of faction. A common passion or interest will, in almost every case, be felt by a majority of the whole; a communication and concert result from the form of government itself; and there is nothing to check the inducements to sacrifice the weaker party or an obnoxious individual. Hence it is that such democracies have ever been spectacles of turbulence and contention; have ever been found incompatible with personal security or the rights of property; and have in general been as short in their lives as they have been violent in their deaths. Theoretic politicians, who have patronized this species of government, have erroneously supposed that by reducing mankind to a perfect equality in their political rights, they would, at the same time, be perfectly equalized and assimilated in their possessions, their opinions, and their passions.

A republic, by which I mean a government in which the scheme of representation takes place, opens a different prospect, and promises the cure for which we are seeking. Let us examine the points in which it varies from pure democracy, and we shall comprehend both the nature of the cure and the efficacy which it must derive from the Union.

The two great points of difference between a democracy and a republic are: first, the delegation of the government, in the latter, to a small number of citizens elected by the rest; secondly, the greater number of citizens, and greater sphere of country, over which the latter may be extended.

The effect of the first difference is, on the one hand, to refine and enlarge the public views, by passing them through the medium of a chosen body of citizens, whose wisdom may best discern the true interest of their country, and whose patriotism and love of justice will be least likely to sacrifice it to temporary or partial considerations. Under such a regulation, it may well happen that the public voice, pronounced by the representatives of the people, will be more consonant to the public good than if pronounced by the people themselves, convened for the purpose. On the other hand, the effect may be inverted. Men of factious tempers, of local prejudices, or of sinister designs, may, by intrigue, by corruption, or by other means, first obtain the suffrages, and then betray the interests, of the people. The question resulting is, whether small or extensive republics are more favorable to the election of proper guardians of the public weal; and it is clearly decided in favor of the latter. . . .

. . . as each representative will be chosen by a greater number of citizens in the large than in the small republic, it will be more difficult for unworthy candidates to practice with success the vicious arts by which elections are too often carried; and the suffrages of the people being more free, will be more likely to centre in men who possess the most attractive merit and the most diffusive and established characters. . . .

The other point of difference is, the greater number of citizens and extent of territory which may be brought within the compass of republican than of democratic government; and it is this circumstance principally which renders factious combinations less to be dreaded in the former than in the latter. The smaller the society, the fewer probably will be the distinct parties and interests composing it; the fewer the distinct parties and interests, the more frequently will a majority be found of the same party; and the smaller the number of individuals composing a majority, and the smaller the compass within which they are placed, the more easily will they concert and execute their plans of oppression. Extend the sphere, and you take in a greater variety of parties and interests; you make it less probable that a majority of the whole will have a common motive to invade the rights of other citizens; or if such a common motive exists, it will be more difficult for all who feel it to discover their own strength, and to act in unison with each other. Besides other impediments, it may be remarked that, where there is a consciousness of unjust or dishonorable purposes, communication is always checked by distrust in proportion to the number whose concurrence is necessary.

Hence, it clearly appears, that the same advantage which a republic has over a democracy, in controlling the effects of faction, is enjoyed by a large over a small republic,—is enjoyed by the Union over the States composing it. Does the advantage consist in the substitution of representatives whose enlightened views and virtuous sentiments render them superior to local prejudices and schemes of injustice? It will not be denied that the representation of the Union will be most likely to possess these requisite endowments. Does it consist in the greater security afforded by a greater variety of parties, against the event of any one party being able to outnumber and oppress the rest? In an equal degree does the increased variety of parties comprised within the Union, increase this security. Does it, in fine, consist in the greater obstacles opposed to the concert and accomplishment of the secret wishes of an unjust and interested majority? Here, again, the extent of the Union gives it the most palpable advantage.

The influence of factious leaders may kindle a flame within their particular States, but will be unable to spread a general conflagration through the other States. A religious sect may degenerate into a political faction in a part of the Confederacy; but the variety of sects dispersed over the entire face of it must secure the national councils against any danger from that source. A rage for paper money, for an abolition of debts, for an equal division of property, or for any other improper or wicked project, will be less apt to pervade the whole body of the Union than a particular member of it; in the same proportion as such a malady is more likely to taint a particular county or district, than an entire State.

In the extent and proper structure of the Union, therefore, we behold a republican remedy for the diseases most incident to republican government. And according to the degree of pleasure and pride we feel in being republicans, ought to be our zeal in cherishing the spirit and supporting the character of Federalists.

DRAWING CONCLUSION:

1. What does the argument presented in Federalist No. 10 reveal about Madison's overall political views?

2.5 JAMES MADISON, "FEDERALIST NO. 51" (1788)

Among the most notable features of the US Constitution was the so-called division of powers or, as it is sometimes called, the "checks and balances." The division of powers takes a number of forms. Power, for instance, is divided between the state and federal governments. The powers of the federal government are divided among three branches (legislative, executive, and judicial). The legislative power is divided between two houses (the House of Representatives and the Senate). In fact, under the Constitution, political authority in the United States is more deeply divided among different levels and branches of government than is the case in most other representative democracies. Scholars have long debated the motivation for this division of powers in the US Constitution, with some arguing that it is designed to protect the people from the abuses of government while others maintaining that it was intended to shield government from the influence of popular opinion. In Federalist No. 51, Madison both makes the case for the division of powers and explains how best, in his view, to achieve it. What goal or goals does Madison say the division of powers serves?

GUIDING QUESTIONS:

1. How does Madison say a division of powers should be accomplished?
2. Why does Madison say a division of powers is necessary?

FEDERALIST NO. 51

THE STRUCTURE OF THE GOVERNMENT MUST FURNISH THE PROPER CHECKS AND BALANCES BETWEEN THE DIFFERENT DEPARTMENTS

JAMES MADISON

To the People of the State of New York:

TO WHAT expedient, then, shall we finally resort, for maintaining in practice the necessary partition of power among the several departments, as laid down in the Constitution? The only answer that can be given is, that as all these exterior provisions are found to be inadequate, the defect must be supplied, by so contriving the interior structure of the government as that its several constituent parts may, by their mutual relations, be the means of keeping each other in their proper places. Without presuming to undertake a full development of this important idea, I will hazard a few general observations, which may perhaps place it in a clearer light, and enable us to form a more correct judgment of the principles and structure of the government planned by the convention.

In order to lay a due foundation for that separate and distinct exercise of the different powers of government, which to a certain extent is admitted on all hands to be essential to the preservation of liberty, it is evident that each department should have a will of its own; and consequently should be so constituted that the members of each should have as little agency as possible in the appointment of the members of the others. Were this principle rigorously adhered to, it would require that all the appointments for the supreme executive, legislative, and judiciary magistracies should be drawn from the same fountain of authority, the people, through channels having no communication whatever with one another. Perhaps such a plan of constructing the several departments would be less difficult in practice than it may in contemplation appear. Some difficulties, however, and some additional expense would attend the execution of it. Some deviations, therefore, from the principle must be admitted. In the constitution of the judiciary department in particular, it might be inexpedient to insist rigorously on the principle: first, because peculiar qualifications being essential in the members, the primary consideration ought to be to select that mode of choice which best secures these qualifications; secondly, because the permanent tenure by which the appointments are held in that department, must soon destroy all sense of dependence on the authority conferring them.

It is equally evident, that the members of each department should be as little dependent as possible on those of the others, for the emoluments annexed to their offices. Were the executive magistrate, or the judges, not independent of the legislature in this particular, their independence in every other would be merely nominal.

But the great security against a gradual concentration of the several powers in the same department, consists in giving to those who administer each department the necessary constitutional means and personal motives to resist encroachments of the others. The provision for defense must in this, as in all other cases, be made commensurate to the danger of attack. Ambition must be made to counteract ambition. The interest of the man must be connected with the constitutional rights of the place. It may be a reflection on human nature, that such devices should be necessary to control the abuses of government. But what is government itself, but the greatest of all reflections on human nature? If men were angels, no government would be necessary. If angels were to govern men, neither external nor internal controls on government would be necessary. In framing a government which is to be administered by men over men, the great difficulty lies in this: you must first enable the government to control the governed; and in the next place oblige it to control itself. A dependence on the people is, no doubt, the primary control on the government; but experience has taught mankind the necessity of auxiliary precautions.

This policy of supplying, by opposite and rival interests, the defect of better motives, might be traced through the whole system of human affairs, private as well as public. We see it particularly displayed in all the subordinate distributions of power, where the constant aim is to divide and arrange the several offices in such a manner as that each may be a check on the other that the private interest of every individual may be a sentinel over the public rights. These inventions of prudence cannot be less requisite in the distribution of the supreme powers of the State.

But it is not possible to give to each department an equal power of self-defense. In republican government, the legislative authority necessarily predominates. The remedy for this inconveniency is to divide the legislature into different branches; and to render them, by different modes of election and different principles of action, as little connected with each other as the nature of their common functions and their common dependence on the society will admit. It may even be necessary to guard against dangerous encroachments by still further precautions. As the weight of the legislative authority requires that it should be thus divided, the weakness of the executive may require, on the other hand, that it should be fortified. An absolute negative on the legislature appears, at first view, to be the natural defense with which the executive magistrate should be armed. But perhaps it would be neither altogether safe nor alone sufficient. On ordinary occasions it might not be exerted with the requisite firmness, and on extraordinary occasions it might be perfidiously abused. May not this defect of an absolute negative be supplied by some qualified connection between this weaker department and the weaker branch of the stronger department, by which the latter may be led to support the constitutional rights of the former, without being too much detached from the rights of its own department?

If the principles on which these observations are founded be just, as I persuade myself they are, and they be applied as a criterion to the several State constitutions, and to the federal Constitution it will be found that if the latter does not perfectly correspond with them, the former are infinitely less able to bear such a test.

There are, moreover, two considerations particularly applicable to the federal system of America, which place that system in a very interesting point of view.

First. In a single republic, all the power surrendered by the people is submitted to the administration of a single government; and the usurpations are guarded against by a division of the government into distinct and separate departments. In the compound republic of America, the power surrendered by the people is first divided between two distinct governments, and then the portion allotted to each subdivided among distinct and separate departments. Hence a double security arises to the rights of the people. The different governments will control each other, at the same time that each will be controlled by itself.

Second. It is of great importance in a republic not only to guard the society against the oppression of its rulers, but to guard one part of the society against the injustice of the other part. Different interests necessarily exist in different classes of citizens. If a majority be united by a common interest, the rights of the minority will be insecure. There are but two methods of providing against this evil: the one by creating a will in the community independent of the majority that is, of the society itself; the other, by comprehending in the society so many separate descriptions of citizens as will render an unjust combination of a majority of the whole very improbable, if not impracticable. The first method prevails in all governments possessing an hereditary or self-appointed authority. This, at best, is but a precarious security; because a power independent of the society may as well espouse the unjust views of the major, as the rightful interests of the minor party, and may possibly be turned against both parties. The second method will be exemplified in the federal republic of the United States. Whilst all authority in it will be derived from and dependent on the society, the society itself will be broken into so many parts, interests, and classes of citizens, that the rights of individuals, or of the minority, will be in little danger from interested combinations of the majority. In a free government the security for civil rights must be the same as that for religious rights. It consists in the one case in the multiplicity of interests, and in the other in the multiplicity of sects. The degree of security in both cases will depend on the number of interests and sects; and this may be presumed to depend on the extent of country and number of people comprehended under the same government. This view of the subject must particularly recommend a proper federal system to all the sincere and considerate friends of republican government, since it shows that in exact proportion as the territory of the Union may be formed into more circumscribed Confederacies, or States oppressive combinations of a majority will be facilitated: the best security, under the republican forms, for the rights of every class of citizens, will be diminished: and consequently the stability and independence of some member of the government, the only other security, must be proportionately increased. Justice is the end of government. It is the end of civil society. It ever has been and ever will be pursued until it be obtained, or until liberty be lost in the pursuit. In a society under the forms of which the stronger faction can readily unite and oppress the weaker, anarchy may as truly be said to reign as in a state of nature, where the weaker individual is not secured against the violence of the stronger; and as, in the latter state, even the stronger individuals are prompted, by the uncertainty of their condition, to submit to a government which may protect the weak as well as themselves; so, in the former state, will the more powerful factions or parties be gradually induced, by a like motive, to wish for a government which will protect all parties, the weaker as well as the more powerful. It can be little doubted that if the State of Rhode Island was separated from the Confederacy and left to itself, the insecurity of rights under the popular form of government within such narrow limits would be displayed by such reiterated oppressions of factious majorities that some power altogether independent of the people would soon be called for by the voice of the very factions whose misrule had proved the necessity of it. In the extended republic of the United States, and among the great variety of interests, parties, and sects which it embraces, a coalition of a majority of the whole society could seldom take place on any other principles than those of justice and the general good; whilst there being thus less danger to a minor from the will of a major party, there must be less pretext, also, to provide for the security of the former, by introducing into the government a will not dependent on the latter, or, in other words, a will independent of the society itself. It is no less certain than it is important, notwithstanding the contrary opinions which have been entertained, that the larger the society, provided it lie within a practical sphere, the more duly capable it will be of self-government. And happily for the *republican cause,* the practicable sphere may be carried to a very great extent, by a judicious modification and mixture of the *federal principle.*

DRAWING CONCLUSION:

1. What does the argument presented in Federalist No. 51 reveal about Madison's overall political views?

DOCUMENTS FROM
SHAYS' REBELLION

The debates over ratification of the Constitution did not happen in a vacuum. When Madison, for instance, spoke of the dangers of faction, he very much had in mind the divisive political battles over issues like paper money and debt relief that had embroiled states like Rhode Island, which culminated in Shays' Rebellion. A deeper examination of Shays' Rebellion can therefore provide insight into the thinking of Federalists such as Madison.

3.1 DANIEL GRAY, "AN ADDRESS TO THE PEOPLE OF THE SEVERAL TOWNS IN THE COUNTY OF HAMPSHIRE, NOW AT ARMS" (1786) AND THOMAS GROVER, "TO THE PRINTER OF THE HAMPSHIRE HERALD" (1786)

In August of 1786, armed bands began to shut down court proceedings in several counties in western Massachusetts to prevent legal action aimed at collecting debts from hard-pressed farmers. When state officials took steps to reopen the courts (included issuing arrest warrants for the protest ringleaders), rebels led by Revolutionary War veteran Daniel Shays launched an armed revolt against the state government. In these documents, rebel leaders Daniel Gray and Thomas Grover summarize the grievances of the rebels.

GUIDING QUESTIONS:

1. What are the specific grievances of Daniel Gray and Thomas Grover?
2. What do these particular grievances reveal about the underlying concerns of the Massachusetts rebels?

"AN ADDRESS TO THE PEOPLE OF THE SEVERAL TOWNS IN THE COUNTY OF HAMPSHIRE, NOW AT ARMS.

"GENTLEMEN,

"We have thought proper to inform you of some of the principal causes of the late risings of the people, and also of their present movement, viz.

"1st. The present expensive mode of collecting debts, which by reason of the great scarcity of cash, will of necessity fill our gaols with unhappy debtors, and thereby a reputable body of people rendered incapable of being serviceable either to themselves or the community.

"2d. The monies raised by impost and excise being appropriated to discharge the interest of governmental securities, and not the foreign debt, when these securities are not subject to taxation.

"3d. A suspension of the writ of *Habeas corpus*, by which those persons who have stepped forth to assert and maintain the rights of the people, are liable to be taken and conveyed even to the most distant part of the Commonwealth, and thereby subjected to an unjust punishment.

"4th. The unlimited power granted to Justices of the Peace and Sheriffs, Deputy Sheriffs, and Constables, by the Riot Act, indemnifying them to the prosecution thereof; when perhaps, wholly actuated from a principle of revenge, hatred, and envy.

"*Furthermore*, Be assured, that this body, now at arms, despise the idea of being instigated by British emissaries, which is so strenuously propagated by the enemies of our liberties: And also wish the most proper and speedy measures may be taken, to discharge both our foreign and domestic debt.

From George Richards Minot, *History of the Insurrection in Massachusetts in 1786 and the Rebellion Consequent Thereon* (Worcester, MA: Isaiah Thomas, 1788), 83–87.

"Per Order,

"DANIEL GRAY, *Chairman of the Committee, for the above purpose.*"

"TO THE PRINTER OF THE HAMPSHIRE HERALD,

"SIR,

"It has some how or other fallen to my lot to be employed in a more conspicuous manner than some others of my fellow citizens, in stepping forth in defence of the rights and privileges of the people, more especially of the county of *Hampshire*.

"THEREFORE, upon the desire of the people now at arms, I take this method to publish to the world of mankind in general, particularly the people of this commonwealth, some of the principal grievances we complain of, and of which we are now seeking redress, and mean to contend for until a redress can be obtained, which we hope will soon take place; and if so our brethren in this commonwealth, that do not see with us as yet, shall find we shall be as peaceable as they be.

"In the first place I must refer you to a draught of grievances drawn up by a Committee of the people now at arms, under the signature of *Daniel Gray*, chairman, which is heartily approved of, some others are also here added, viz.

"1st. The General Court, for certain obvious reasons, must be removed out of the town of Boston.

"2d. A revision of the constitution is absolutely necessary.

"3d. All kinds of governmental securities, now on interest, that have been bought of the original owners, for two shillings, three shillings, four shillings, and the highest for six shillings and eight pence on the pound, and have received more interest than ever the principal cost the speculator who purchased them—that if justice was done, we verily believe nay positively know, it would save this Commonwealth thousands of pounds.

"4th. Let the lands belonging to this Commonwealth at the eastward, be sold at the best advantage, to pay the remainder of our domestic debt.

"5th. Let the monies arising from impost and excise, be appropriated to discharge the foreign debt.

"6th. Let that act, passed by the General Court last *June*, by a small majority of only seven, called the Supplementary Aid, for twenty-five years yet to come, be repealed.

"7th. The total abolition of the Inferior Court of Common Pleas and General Sessions of the Peace.

"8th. Deputy Sheriffs totally set aside, as a useless set of officers in the community; and Constables, who are really necessary, be impowered to do the duty, by which means a large swarm of lawyers will be banished form their wonted haunts, who have been more damage to the people at large, especially the common farmers, than the savage beasts of prey.

"To this I boldly sign my proper name, as a hearty well wisher to the real rights of the people.

"THOMAS GROVER.

"*Worcester, December 7, 1786.*

DRAWING CONCLUSIONS:

1. What can we learn about the social conflicts of the 1780s from the grievances of the Massachusetts rebels?

2. What insights can this provide into the ideas advocated by Federalists like Hamilton and Madison in the documents that they authored?

ANTI-FEDERALIST DOCUMENTS

The arguments advanced by anti-Federalists, of course, provide no direct evidence of the motives of the Federalists, nor do anti-Federalist claims that the proposed constitution was "aristocratic" prove that it actually was. An examination of anti-Federalist documents, however, can provide a sense of the controversies surrounding constitutional ratification and provide a context for the ideas advanced by Federalists like Hamilton and Madison.

4.1   ESSAY BY MONTEZUMA (1787)

In this essay, published in a Philadelphia newspaper in October 1787, an anti-Federalist writing under the pen name "Montezuma" offers a parody of the Federalists. Speaking on behalf of the "Aristocratic party of the United States," Montezuma presents a satiric, pro-ratification argument. In doing so, Montezuma portrays the proposed constitution as the product of a conspiracy of the "well-born" against the "rabble."

GUIDING QUESTIONS:

1. How does Montezuma portray the motives of the Federalists?
2. What specific provisions of the proposed constitution does Montezuma cite as evidence of these motives?

We the Aristocratic party of the United States, lamenting the many inconveniences to which the late confederation subjected the *well-born*, the better kind of people, bringing them down to the level of the *rabble*, and holding in utter detestation that frontispiece to every bill of rights, "that all men are born equal," beg leave (for the purpose of drawing a line between such as we think were *ordained* to govern, and such as were *made* to bear the weight of government without having any share in its administration) to submit to *our friends* in the first class for their inspection, the following defense of our *monarchical, aristocratical democracy*.

lst. As a majority of all societies consist of men who (though totally incapable of thinking or acting in governmental matters) are more readily led than driven, we have thought meet to indulge them in something like a democracy in the new constitution, which part we have designated by the popular name of the House of Representatives; but to guard against every possible danger from this *lower house*, we have subjected every bill they bring forward, to the double negative of our *upper house* and president—nor have we allowed the *populace* the right to elect their representatives annually . . . lest this body should be too much under the influence and control of their constituents, and thereby prove the "weatherboard of our grand edifice, to show the shiftings of every fashionable gale," for we have not yet to learn that little else is wanting to aristocratize the most democratical representative than to make him somewhat independent of his *political creators*—We have taken away that rotation of appointment which has so long perplexed us—that *grand engine* of popular influence; every man is eligible into our government, from time to time for life—this will have a two-fold good effect; first, it prevents the representatives from mixing with the *lower class*, and imbibing their foolish sentiments, with which they would have come charged on re-election.

2d. They will from the perpetuality of office be under *our* eye, and in a short time will think and act like *us*, independently of popular whims and prejudices; for the assertion "that evil communications corrupt good manners," is not more true than its reverse. We have allowed this house the power to impeach, but we have tenaciously reserved the right to try. We hope gentlemen, you will see the policy of this clause—for what matters it who accuses, if the accused is tried by his friends—In fine, this *plebian*

From Herbert J. Storing, ed., *The Complete Anti-Federalist*, vol. 3 (Chicago: University of Chicago Press, 1981), 53–57.

house will have little power, and that little be rightly shaped by our house of *gentlemen,* who will have a very extensive influence, from their being chosen out of the *genteeler class,* and their appointment being almost a life, one as seven years is the calculation on a man's life, and they are chosen for six; It is true, every third senatorial seat is to be vacated duennually, but two-thirds of this influential body will remain in office, and be ready to direct or (if necessary) bring over to the good old way, the young members, if the old ones should not be returned; and whereas many of our brethren, from a laudable desire to support their rank in life above the commonalty, have not only deranged their finances, but subjected their persons to indecent treatment (as being arrested for debt, etc.) we have framed a privilege clause, by which they may laugh at the fools who trusted them; but we have given out, that this clause was provided, only that the members might be able without interruption, to deliberate on the important business of their country.

We have frequently endeavored to effect in our respective states, the happy discrimination which pervades this system, but finding we could not bring the states into it individually, we have determined, and in this our general plan we have taken pains to leave the legislature of each *free* and *independent* state, as they now call themselves, in such a situation that they will eventually be absorbed by our *grand continental vortex,* or dwindle into petty corporations, and have power over little else than *yoking hogs* or determining the width of *cart wheels*—but (aware that an intention to annihilate state legislatures, would be objected to our favorite scheme) we have made their existence (as a *board of electors*) necessary to ours; this furnishes us and our advocates with a fine answer to any clamors that may be raised on this subject, viz.— We have so interwoven continental and state legislatures that they cannot exist separately; whereas we in truth, only leave them the power of electing us, for what can a provincial legislature do when we possess "the exclusive regulation of external and internal commerce, excise, duties, imposts, post-offices and roads["]; when we and we alone, have the power to wage war, make peace, coin money (if we can get bullion) if not, borrow money, organize the militia

and call them forth to execute our decrees, and crush insurrections assisted by a noble body of veterans subject to our nod, which we have the power of raising and keeping even in the time of peace. What have we to fear from state legislatures or even from states, when we are armed with such powers, with a president at our head? (a name we thought proper to adopt in conformity to the prejudices of a silly people who are so foolishly fond of a Republican government, that we were obliged to accommodate in names and forms to them, in order more effectually to secure the substance of our proposed plan; but we all know that Cromwell was a King, with the title of protector). I repeat it, what have we to fear armed with such powers, with a president at our head who is captain-general of the army, navy and militia of the United States, who can make and unmake treaties, appoint and commission ambassadors and other ministers, who can grant or refuse reprieves or pardons, who can make judges of the supreme and other continental courts, in short who will be the source, the fountain of honor, profit and power, whose influence like the rays of the sun, will diffuse itself far and wide, will exhale all *democratical vapors* and break the *clouds of popular insurrection*? But again gentlemen, our judicial power is a strong work, a masked battery, few people see the guns we can and will ere long play off from it; for the judicial power embraces every question which can arise in law or equity, under this constitution and under the laws of "the United States"— (which laws will be, you know, the supreme laws of the land)—This power extends to all cases, affecting ambassadors or other public ministers, "and consuls to all cases of admiralty and maritime jurisdiction— to controversies to which the United States shall be a party, to controversies between two or more States, between a State and citizens of another State, between citizens of different States, between citizens of the same State, claiming lands under grants of different States; and between a State or the citizens thereof, and foreign States, citizens or subjects."

Now, can a question arise in the colonial courts, which the ingenuity or sophistry of an able lawyer may not bring within one or other of the above cases? Certainly not. Then our court will have original or appellate jurisdiction in all cases—and if so, how fallen are state judicatures—and must not every provincial law yield to our supreme flat? Our constitution answers yes—then how insignificant the makers of these laws be—it is in the nature of power to create influence—and finally we shall entrench ourselves so as to laugh at the cabals of the commonalty—a few regiments will do at first; it must be spread abroad that they are absolutely necessary to defend the frontiers. Now a regiment and then a legion must be added quietly; bye and bye a frigate or two must be built, still taking care to intimate that they are essential to the support of our revenue laws and to prevent smuggling. We have said nothing about a bill of rights, for we viewed it as an eternal clog upon our designs—as a lock chain to the wheels of government—though, by the way, as we have not insisted on rotation in our offices, the simile of a wheel is ill. We have for some time considered the freedom of the press as a great evil—It spreads information, and begets a licentiousness in the people which needs the rein more than the spur; besides, a daring printer may expose the plans of government and lessen the consequence of our president and senate; for these and many other reasons we have said nothing with respect to the "right of the people to speak and publish their sentiments," or about their "palladiums of liberty," and such stuff. We do not much like that sturdy privilege of the people—the right to demand the writ of *habeas corpus*—we have therefore reserved the power of refusing it in cases of rebellion, and you know we are the judges of what is rebellion. Things as yet are well—Our friends we find have been assiduous in representing our federal calamities, until at length the people at large frightened by the gloomy picture on one side, and allured by the prophecies of some of our fanciful and visionary adherents on the other, are ready to accept and confirm our proposed government without the delay or forms of examination, which was the more to be wished, as they are wholly unfit to investigate the principles or pronounce on the merit of so exquisite a system. Impressed with a conviction that this constitution is calculated to restrain the influence and power of the LOWER CLASS—to draw that *discrimination* we have so long sought after; to secure to our friends *privileges and offices*, which were not to be valued on under the former government, because they were in common—to take the burden of *legislation and attendance on public business* off the commonalty, who will be much better able thereby to prosecute with effect their private business, to destroy that *political thirteen headed monster*, the state sovereignties, to check the *licentiousness* of the people by making it dangerous to *speak or publish* daring or tumultuary sentiments, to enforce obedience to laws by a *strong executive*, aided by *military pensioners*, and finally to promote the public and private interests of the *better kind* of people. We submit it to your judgment to take such measures for its adoption as you in your wisdom may think fit.

Signed by unanimous order of the lords spiritual and temporal.
Montezuma, President

DRAWING CONCLUSION:

1. What can we learn from Montezuma's essay about the concerns of anti-Federalists?

4.2 "POLITICAL CREED
OF EVERY FEDERALIST" (1787)

In December 1787, a newspaper in New York published this brief parody of the pro-ratification forces in which the anonymous author provides a brief satiric summary of the purported political beliefs of the Federalists. While the document lacks any detailed discussion of the specific provisions of the proposed constitution, it is an excellent example of how many anti-Federalists viewed the pro-constitution forces.

GUIDING QUESTIONS:

1. What political views does the author attribute to the Federalists?
2. What overall portrait does the author paint of the Federalists?

BELIEVE in the infallibility, all sufficient wisdom, and infinite goodness of the late convention; or, in other words, I believe that some men are of so perfect a nature that it is absolutely impossible for them to commit errors or design villainy.

I believe that the great body of the people are incapable of judging in their nearest concerns, and that, therefore, they ought to be guided by the opinions of their superiors.

I believe that it is totally unnecessary to secure the rights of mankind in the formation of a constitution,

I believe that aristocracy is the best form of government.

I believe that the people of America are cowards and unable to defend themselves and that, consequently, standing armies are absolutely necessary.

I believe that trial by jury, and the freedom of the press ought to be exploded from every wise government.

I believe that the new constitution will not affect the state constitutions, yet that the state officers will oppose it, because it will abridge their power.

I believe that the new constitution will prove the bulwark of liberty—the balm of misery—the essence of justice—and the astonishment of mankind. In short, I believe (in the words of that admirable reasoner, Attorney Wilson) that it is the best form of government which has ever been offered to the world.

I believe that to speak, write, read, think, or hear any thing against the proposed government, is damnable heresy, execrable rebellion, and high treason against the sovereign majesty of the convention—And lastly, I believe that every person, who differs from me in belief, is an infernal villain. AMEN.

DRAWING CONCLUSION:

1. What can we learn from this document about the concerns of anti-Federalists?

"Political Creed of Every Federalist," *New York Journal and Weekly Register*, December 2, 1787.

4.3 MERCY OTIS WARREN, "OBSERVATIONS ON THE NEW CONSTITUTION, AND ON THE FEDERAL AND STATE CONVENTIONS BY A COLUMBIAN PATRIOT" (1788)

Although women were excluded from formal leadership roles in the movement for American independence, many were active in the movement in such varied roles as organizers, strategists, and spokespeople. Among the most prominent of these patriot women was Mercy Otis Warren. Warren (whose father, husband, and brother were all prominent public figures in Massachusetts and critics of British rule) was an outspoken advocate for independence, having anonymously published a series of revolutionary poems and plays. In 1788, again writing under a pen name (a "Columbian Patriot") she published a pamphlet (entitled "Observations on the New Constitution, And on the Federal and State Conventions") in which she critiqued the proposed constitution and urged its rejection. Though Warren's argument echoed those of other anti-Federalists, she couched her position in deeper historical and philosophical terms and employs a literary style that, at times, may make her writing more challenging than that of other anti-Federalists. As you read Warren, focus on those sections of the document where she most clearly presents what she considers to be the flaws of the proposed constitution.

GUIDING QUESTIONS:

1. What specific defects does Warren identify in the proposed constitution?
2. What is her overall view of the proposed constitution?

OBSERVATIONS ON THE NEW CONSTITUTION, AND ON THE FEDERAL AND STATE CONVENTIONS

By a Columbian Patriot
Boston 1788

Sic transit gloria Americana,

Mankind may amuse themselves with theoretick systems of liberty, and trace its social and moral effects on sciences, virtue, industry and every improvement of which the human mind is capable; but we can only discern its true value by the practical and wretched effects of slavery; and thus dreadfully will they be realized, when the inhabitants of the Eastern States are dragging out a miserable existence, *only* on the gleanings of their fields; and the Southern, blessed with a softer and more fertile climate, are languishing in hopeless poverty; and when asked, what is become of the flower of their crop, and the rich produce of their farms—they may answer in the hapless stile of the Man of La Mancha,—"The steward of my Lord has seized and sent it to *Madrid.*" Or, in the more literal language of truth, The *exigencies* of government require that the collectors of the revenue should transmit it to the *Federal City.*

Animated with the firmest zeal for the interest of this country, the peace and union of the American States, and the freedom and happiness of a people who have made the most costly sacrifices in the cause of liberty,—who have braved the power of Britain, weathered the convulsions of war, and waded thro' the blood of friends and foes to establish their independence and to support the freedom of the human mind; I cannot silently witness this degradation without calling on them, before they are compelled to blush at their own servitude, and to turn back their languid eyes on their lost liberties—to consider, that the character of nations generally changes at the moment of revolution.—And when patriotism is discountenanced and publick virtue becomes the ridicule of the sycophant—when every man of liberality, firmness and penetration who cannot lick the hand stretched out to oppress, is deemed an enemy to the State—then is the gulph of despotism set open, and the grades to slavery, though rapid, are scarce perceptible—then genius drags heavily its iron chain—science is neglected, and real merit flies to the shades for security from reproach—the mind becomes enervated, and the national character sinks to a kind of apathy with only energy sufficient to curse the breast that gave it milk, and as an elegant writer observes, "To bewail every new birth as an increase of misery, under a government where the mind is necessarily debased, and talents are seduced to become the panegyrists of usurpation and tyranny." He adds, "that even sedition is not the most indubitable enemy to the publick welfare; but that its most dreadful foe is despotism which always changes the character of nations for the worse, and is productive of nothing but vice, that the tyrant no longer excites to the pursuits of glory or virtue; it is not talents, it is baseness and servility that he cherishes, and the weight of arbitrary power destroys the spring of emulation." If such is the influence of government on the character and manners, and undoubtedly the observation is just, must we not subscribe to the opinion of the celebrated *Abbé Mablé*? "That there are disagreeable seasons in the unhappy situation of human affairs, when policy requires both the intention and the power of doing mischief to be punished; and when the senate proscribed the memory of Caesar they ought to have put Anthony to death, and extinguished the hopes of *Octavius*." Self defence is a primary law of nature, which no subsequent law of society can abolish; this primaeval principle, the immediate gift of the Creator, obliges every one to remonstrate against the strides of ambition, and a wanton lust of domination, and to resist the first approaches of tyranny, which at this day threaten to sweep away the rights for which the brave Sons of America have fought with an heroism scarcely paralleled even in ancient republicks.

It may be repeated, they have purchased it with their blood, and have gloried in their independence with a dignity of spirit, which has made them the admiration of philosophy, the pride of America, and the wonder of Europe. It has been observed, with great propriety, that "the virtues and vices of a people" when a revolution happens in their government, are the measure of the liberty or slavery they ought to expect—An heroic love for the publick good, a profound reverence for the laws, a contempt of riches, and a noble haughtiness of "soul, are the only foundations of a free government." Do not their dignified principles still exist among us? Or are they extinguished in the breasts of Americans, whose fields have been so recently crimsoned to repel the potent arm of a foreign Monarch, who had planted his engines of slavery in every city, with design to erase the vestiges of freedom in this his last asylum. It is yet to be hoped, for the honour of human nature, that no combinations either foreign or domestick have thus darkened this Western hemisphere.— On these shores freedom has planted her standard, dipped in the purple tide that flowed from the veins of her martyred heroes; and here every uncorrupted American yet hopes to see it supported by the vigour, the justice, the wisdom and unanimity of the people, in spite of the deep-laid plots the secret intrigues, or the bold effrontery of those interested and avaricious adventurers for place, who intoxicated with the ideas of distinction and preferment have prostrated every worthy principle beneath the shrine of ambition. Yet these are the men who tell us republicanism is dwindled into theory—that we are incapable of enjoying our liberties—and that we must have a master.—Let us retrospect the days of our adversity, and recollect who were then our friends; do we find them among the sticklers for aristocratick authority? No, they were generally the same men who now wish to save us from the distractions of anarchy on the one hand, and the jaws of tyranny on the other; where then were the class who now come forth importunately urging that our political salvation depends on the adoption of a system at which freedom spurns?—Were not some of them hidden in the corners of obscurity, and others wrapping themselves in the bosom of our enemies for safety? Some of them were in the arms of infancy; and others speculating for fortune, by sporting with public

money; while a few, a very few of them were magnani-
mously defending their country, and raising a character, which I pray heaven may never be sullied by
aiding measures derogatory to their former exertions.
But the revolutions in principle which time produces
among mankind, frequently exhibits the most mortifying instances of human weakness; and this alone
can account for the extraordinary appearance of a few
names, once distinguished in the honourable walks
of patriotism, but now found in the list of the Massachusetts assent to the ratification of a Constitution,
which, by the undefined meaning of some parts, and
the ambiguities of expression in others, is dangerously
adapted to the purposes of an immediate *aristocratic
tyranny*; that from the difficulty, if not impracticability of its operation, must soon terminate in the most
uncontrouled despotism.

All writers on government agree, and the feelings
of the human mind witness the truth of these political axioms, that man is born free and possessed of
certain unalienable rights—that government is instituted for the protection, safety and happiness of
the people, and not for the profit, honour, or private
interest of any man, family, or class of men—That
the origin of all power is in the people, and that they
have an incontestible right to check the creatures of
their own creation, vested with certain powers to
guard the life, liberty and property of the community: And if certain selected bodies of men, deputed
on these principles, determine contrary to the wishes
and expectations of their constituents, the people
have an undoubted right to reject their decisions, to
call for a revision of their conduct, to depute others
in their room, or if they think proper, to demand
further time for deliberation on matters of the greatest moment: it therefore is an unwarrantable stretch
of authority or influence, if any methods are taken
to preclude this peaceful and reasonable mode of
enquiry and decision. And it is with inexpressible
anxiety, that many of the best friends of the Union
of the States—to the peaceable and equal participation of the rights of nature, and to the glory and dignity of this country, behold the insidious arts, and
the strenuous efforts of the partisans of arbitrary
power, by their vague definitions of the best established truths, endeavoring to envelope the mind in

darkness the concomitant of slavery, and to lock the
strong chains of domestic despotism on a country,
which by the most glorious and successful struggles
is but newly emancipated from the spectre of foreign dominion.—But there are certain seasons in the
course of human affairs, when Genius, Virtue, and
Patriotism, seems to nod over the vices of the times,
and perhaps never more remarkably, than at the
present period; or we should not see such a passive
disposition prevail in some, who we must candidly
suppose, have liberal and enlarged sentiments; while
a supple multitude are paying a blind and idolatrous
homage to the opinions of those who by the most
precipitate steps are treading down their dear bought
privileges; and who are endeavouring by all the arts
of insinuation, and influence, to betray the people
of the United States, into an acceptance of a most
complicated system of government; marked on the
one side with the *dark, secret* and *profound intrigues*, of
the statesman, long practised in the purlieus of despotism; and on the other, with the ideal projects of
young ambition, with its wings just expanded to soar
to a summit, which imagination has painted in such
gawdy colours as to intoxicate the *inexperienced votary*,
and to send him rambling from State to State, to collect materials to construct the ladder of preferment.

But as a variety of objections to the *heteroge-
neous* phantom, have been repeatedly laid before the
public, by men of the best abilities and intentions;
I will not expatiate long on a Republican *form* of government, founded on the principles of monarchy—a
democratick branch with the *features* of aristocracy—
and the extravagance of nobility pervading the minds
of many of the candidates for office, with the poverty of peasantry hanging heavily on them, and insurmountable, from their taste for expence, unless
a general provision should be made in the arrange-
ment of the civil list, which may enable them with
the champions of their cause to "*sail down the new
pactolean channel.*" Some gentlemen, with laboured
zeal, have spent much time in urging the necessity
of government, from the embarrassments of trade—
the want of respectability abroad and confidence of
the public engagements at home:—These are obvious
truths which no one denies; and there are few who
do not unite in the general wish for the restoration

of public faith, the revival of commerce, arts, agriculture, and industry, under a lenient, peaceable and energetick government: But the most sagacious advocates for the party have not by fair discusion, and rational argumentation, evinced the necessity of adopting this many-headed monster; of such motley mixture, that its enemies cannot trace a feature of Democratick or Republican extract; nor have its friends the courage to denominate a Monarchy, an Aristocracy, or an Oligarchy, and the favoured bantling must have passed through the short period of its existence without a name, had not Mr. *Wilson*, in the fertility of his genius, suggested the happy epithet of a *Federal Republic*—But I leave the field of general censure on the secresy of its birth, the rapidity of its growth, and the fatal consequences of suffering it to live to the age of maturity, and will particularize some of the most weighty objections to its passing through this continent in a gigantic size.—It will be allowed by every one that the fundamental principle of a free government is the equal representation of a free people—And I will *first* observe with a justly celebrated writer, "That the principal aim of society is to protect individuals in the absolute rights which were vested in them by the immediate laws of nature, but which could not be preserved in peace, without the mutual intercourse which is gained by the institution of friendly and social communities." And when society has thus deputed a certain number of their equals to take care of their personal rights, and the interest of the whole community, it must be considered that responsibility is the great security of integrity and honour; and that annual election is the basis of responsibility,—Man is not immediately corrupted, but power without limitation, or amenability, may endanger the brightest virtue—whereas frequent return to the bar of their Constituents is the strongest check against the corruptions to which men are liable, either from the intrigues of others of more subtle genius, or the propensities of their own hearts,—and the gentlemen who have so warmly advocated in the late Convention of the Massachusetts, the change from annual to biennial elections; may have been in the same predicament, and perhaps with the same views that Mr. *Hutchinson* once acknowledged himself, when in a letter to *Lord Hillsborough,*

he observed, "that the grand difficulty of making a change in government against the general bent of the people had caused him to turn his thoughts to a variety of plans, in order to find one that might be executed in spite of opposition," and the first he proposed was that, "instead of annual, the elections should be only once in three years:" but the Minister had not the hardiness to attempt such an innovation, even in the revision of colonial charters: nor has any one ever defended Biennial, Triennial or Septennial Elections, either in the British House of Commons, or in the debates of Provincial assemblies, on general and free principles: but it is unnecessary to dwell long on this article, as the best political writers have supported the principles of annual elections with a precision, that cannot be confuted, though they may be darkened, by the sophistical arguments that have been thrown out with design, to undermine all the barriers of freedom.

2. There is no security in the proffered system, either for the rights of conscience or the liberty of the Press: Despotism usually while it is gaining ground, will suffer men to think, say, or write what they please; but when once established, if it is thought necessary to subserve the purposes, of arbitrary power, the most unjust restrictions may take place in the first instance, and an *imprimator* on the Press in the next, may silence the complaints, and forbid the most decent remonstrances of an injured and oppressed people.

3. There are no well defined limits of the Judiciary Powers, they seem to be left as a boundless ocean, that has broken over the chart of the Supreme Lawgiver, *"thus far shalt thou go and no further,"* and as they cannot be comprehended by the clearest capacity, or the most sagacious mind, it would be an Herculean labour to attempt to describe the dangers with which they are replete.

4. The Executive and the Legislative are so dangerously blended as to give just cause of alarm, and everything relative thereto, is couched in such ambiguous terms—in such vague and indefinite expression, as is a sufficient ground without any objection, for the reprobation of a system, that the authors dare not hazard to a clear investigation.

5. The abolition of trial by jury in civil causes.—This mode of trial the learned Judge Blackstone

observes, "has been coeval with the first rudiments of civil government, that property, liberty and life, depend on maintaining in its legal force the constitutional trial by jury." He bids his readers pause, and with Sir Matthew Hale observes, how admirably this mode is adapted to the investigation of truth beyond any other the world can produce. Even the party who have been disposed to swallow, without examination, the proposals of the *secret conclave*, have started on a discovery that this essential right was curtailed; and shall a privilege, the origin of which may be traced to our Saxon ancestors—that has been a part of the law of nations, even in the fewdatory systems of France, Germany and Italy—and from the earliest records has been held so sacred, both in ancient and modern Britain, that it could never be shaken by the introduction of Norman customs, or any other conquests or change of government—shall this inestimable privilege be relinquished in America—either thro' the fear of inquisition for unaccounted thousands of public monies in the hands of some who have been officious in the fabrication of the *consolidated system*, or from the apprehension that some future delinquent possessed of more power than integrity, may be called to a trial by his peers in the hour of investigation?

6. Though it has been said by Mr. *Wilson* and many others, that a Standing-Army is necessary for the dignity and safety of America, yet freedom revolts at the idea, when the Divan, or the Despot, may draw out his dragoons to suppress the murmurs of a few, who may yet cherish those sublime principles which call forth the exertions, and lead to the best improvements of the human mind. It is hoped this country may yet be governed by milder methods than are usually displayed beneath the bannerets of military law.—Standing armies have been the nursery of vice and the bane of liberty from the Roman legions to the establishment of the artful Ximenes, and from the ruin of the Cortes of Spain, to the planting of the British cohorts in the capitals of America:—By the edicts of an authority vested in the sovereign power by the proposed constitution, the militia of the country, the bulwark of defence, and the security of national liberty if no longer under the control of civil authority; but at the rescript of the Monarch, or the aristocracy, they may either be employed to extort the enormous sums that will be necessary to support the civil list— to maintain the regalia of power—and the splendour of the most useless part of the community, or they may be sent into foreign countries for the fulfilment of treaties, stipulated by the President and two-thirds of the Senate.

7. Notwithstanding the delusory promise to guarantee a Republican form of government to every State in the Union—if the most discerning eye could discover any meaning at all in the engagement, there are no resources left for the support of internal government or the liquidation of the debts of the State. Every source of revenue is in the monopoly of Congress, and if the several legislatures in their enfeebled state, should against their own feelings be necessitated to attempt a dry tax for the payment of their debts, and the support of internal police, even this may be required for the purposes of the general government.

8. As the new Congress are empowered to determine their own salaries, the requisitions for this purpose may not be very moderate, and the drain for public moneys will probably rise past all calculation: and it is to be feared when America has consolidated its despotism, the world will witness the truth of the assertion—"that the pomp of an Eastern monarch may impose on the vulgar who may estimate the force of a nation by the magnificence of its palaces; but the wise man judges differently, it is by that very magnificence he estimates its weakness. He sees nothing more in the midst of this imposing pomp, where the tyrant sets enthroned, than a sumptuous and mournful decoration of the dead; the apparatus of a fastuous funeral, in the centre of which is a cold and lifeless lump of unanimated earth, a phantom of power ready to disappear before the enemy, by whom it is despised!"

9. There is no provision for a rotation, nor anything to prevent the perpetuity of office in the same hands for life; which by a little well timed bribery, will probably be done, to the exclusion of men of the best abilities from their share in the offices of government.—By this neglect we lose the advantages of that check to the overbearing insolence of office, which by rendering him ineligible at certain periods, keeps the mind of man in equilibrio, and teaches

him the feelings of the governed, and better qualifies him to govern in his turn.

10. The inhabitants of the United States, are liable to be dragged from the vicinity of their own country, or state, to answer the litigious or unjust suit of an adversary, on the most distant borders of the Continent: in short the appellate jurisdiction of the Supreme Federal Court, includes an unwarrantable stretch of power over the liberty, life, and property of the subject, through the wide Continent of America.

11. One Representative to thirty thousand inhabitants is a very inadequate representation; and every man who is not lost to all sense of freedom to his country, must reprobate the idea of Congress altering by law, or on any pretence whatever, interfering with any regulations for time, places, and manner of choosing our own Representatives.

12. If the sovereignty of America is designed to be elective, the circumscribing the votes to only ten electors in this State, and the same proportion in all the others, is nearly tantamount to the exclusion of the voice of the people in the choice of their first magistrate. It is vesting the choice solely in an aristocratic junto, who may easily combine in each State to place at the head of the Union the most convenient instrument for despotic sway.

13. A Senate chosen for six years will, in most instances, be an appointment for life, as the influence of such a body over the minds of the people will be coequal to the extensive powers with which they are vested, and they will not only forget, but be forgotten by their constituents—a branch of the Supreme Legislature thus set beyond all responsibility is totally repugnant to every principle of a free government.

14. There is no provision by a bill of rights to guard against the dangerous encroachments of power in too many instances to be named: but I cannot pass over in silence the insecurity in which we are left with regard to warrants unsupported by evidence—the daring experiment of granting *writs of assistance* in a former arbitrary administration is not yet forgotten in the Massachusetts; nor can we be so ungrateful to the memory of the patriots who counteracted their operation, as so soon after their manly exertions to save us from such a detestable instrument of arbitrary power, to subject ourselves to the insolence of

any petty revenue officer to enter our houses, search, insult, and seize at pleasure. We are told by a gentleman of too much virtue and real probity to suspect he has a design to deceive—"that the whole constitution is a declaration of rights"—but mankind must think for themselves, and to many very judicious and discerning characters, the whole constitution with very few exceptions appears a perversion of the rights of particular states, and of private citizens. But the gentleman goes on to tell us, "that the primary object is the general government, and that the rights of individuals are only incidentally mentioned, and that there was a clear impropriety in being very particular about them." But, asking pardon for dissenting from such respectable authority, who has been led into several mistakes, more from his predilection in favour of certain modes of government, than from a want of understanding or veracity. The rights of individuals ought to be the primary object of all government, and cannot be too securely guarded by the most explicit declarations in their favor. This has been the opinion of the Hampdens, the Pyms, and many other illustrious names, that have stood forth in defence of English liberties; and even the Italian master in politicks, the subtle and renouned Machiavel acknowledges, that no republic ever yet stood on a stable foundation without satisfying the common people.

15. The difficulty, if not impracticability, of exercising the equal and equitable powers of government by a single legislature over an extent of territory that reaches from the Mississippi to the Western lakes, and from them to the Atlantic Ocean, is an insuperable objection to the adoption of the new system.— Mr. *Hutchinson*, the great champion for arbitrary power, in the multitude of his machinations to subvert the liberties in this country, was obliged to acknowledge in one of his letters, that, "from the extent of country from north to south, the scheme of one government was impracticable." But if the authors of the present visionary project, can by the arts of deception, precipitation and address, obtain a majority of suffrages in the conventions of the states to try the hazardous experiment, they may then make the same inglorious boast with this insidious politician, who may perhaps be their model, that "the union

of the colonies was pretty well broken, and that he hoped to never see it reviewed."

16. It is an undisputed fact that not one legislature in the United States had the most distant idea when they first appointed members for a convention, entirely commercial, or when they afterwards authorized them to consider on some amendments of the Federal union, that they would without any warrant from their constituents, presume on so bold and daring a stride, as ultimately to destroy the state governments, and offer a *consolidated system*, irreversible but on conditions that the smallest degree of penetration must discover to be impracticable.

17. The first appearance of the article which declares the ratification of nine states sufficient for the establishment of the new system, wears the face of dissension, is a subversion of the union of Confederated States, and tends to the introduction of anarchy and civil convulsions, and may be a means of involving the whole country in blood.

18. The mode in which this constitution is recommended to the people to judge without either the advice of Congress, or the legislatures of the several states is very reprehensible—it is an attempt to force it upon them before it could be thoroughly understood, and may leave us in that situation, that in the first moments of slavery in the minds of the people agitated by the remembrance of their lost liberties, will be like the sea in a tempest, that sweeps down every mound of security.

But it is needless to enumerate other instances, in which the proposed constitution appears contradictory to the first principles which ought to govern mankind; and it is equally so to enquire into the motives that induced to so bold a step as the annihilation of the independence and sovereignty of the thirteen distinct states.—They are but too obvious through the whole progress of the business, from the first shutting up the doors of the federal convention and resolving that no member should correspond with gentlemen in the different states on the subject under discussion; till the trivial proposition of *recommending* a few amendments was artfully ushered into the convention of the Massachusetts. The questions that were then before that honorable assembly were profound and important, they were of such

magnitude and extent, that the consequences may run parallel with the existence of the country; and to see them waved and hastily terminated by a measure too absurd to require a serious refutation, raises the honest indignation of every true lover of his country. Nor are they less grieved that the ill policy and arbitrary disposition of some of the sons of America has thus precipitated to the contemplation and discussion of questions that no one could rationally suppose would have been agitated among us, till time had blotted out the principles on which the late revolution was grounded; or till the last traits of the many political tracts, which defended the separation from Britain, and the rights of men were consigned to everlasting oblivion. After the severe conflicts this country has suffered, it is presumed that they are disposed to make every reasonable sacrifice before the altar of peace—But when we contemplate the nature of men and consider them originally on an equal footing, subject to the same feelings, stimulated by the same passions, and recollecting the struggles they have recently made, for the security of their civil rights; it cannot be expected that the inhabitants of the Massachusetts, can be easily lulled into a fatal security, by the declamatory effusions of gentlemen, who, contrary to the experience of all ages would persuade them there is no danger to be apprehended, from vesting discretionary powers in the hands of man, which he may, or may not abuse. The very suggestion, that we ought to trust to the precarious hope of amendments and redress, after we have voluntarily fixed the shackles on our own necks should have awakened to a double, degree of caution.—This people have not forgotten the artful insinuations of a former Governor, when pleading the unlimited authority of parliament before the legislature of the Massachusetts; nor that his arguments were very similar to some lately urged by gentlemen who boast of opposing his measures, *"with halters about their necks."*

We were then told by him, in all the soft language of insinuation, that no form of government, of human construction can be perfect—that we had nothing to fear—that we had no reason to complain—that we had only to acquiesce in their illegal claims, and to submit to the requisition of parliament, and doubtless the lenient hand of government would redress all grievances, and remove the oppressions of the people:—Yet we soon saw armies of mercenaries encamped on our plains—our commerce ruined—our harbours blockaded—and our cities burnt. It maybe replied that this was in consequence of an obstinate defence of our privileges; this may be true; and when the *"ultima ratio"* is called to aid, the weakest must fall. But let the best informed historian produce an instance when bodies of men were entrusted with power, and the proper checks relinquished, if they were ever found destitute of ingenuity sufficient to furnish pretences to abuse it. And the people at large are already sensible, that the liberties which America has claimed, which reason has justified, and which have been so gloriously defended by the swords of the brave; are not about to fall before the tyranny of foreign conquest: it is native usurpation that is shaking the foundations of peace, and spreading the sable curtain of despotism over the United States. The banners of freedom were erected in the wilds of America by our ancestors, while the wolf prowled for his prey on the one hand, and more savage man on the other; they have been since rescued from the invading hand of foreign power, by the valor and blood of their posterity; and there was reason to hope they would continue for ages to illumine a quarter of the globe, by nature kindly separated from the proud monarchies of Europe, and the infernal darkness of Asiatic slavery.—And it is to be feared we shall soon see this country rushing into the extremes of confusion and violence, in consequence of the proceeding of a set of gentlemen, who disregarding the purposes of their appointment, have assumed powers unauthorized by any commission, have unnecessarily rejected the confederation of the United States, and annihilated the sovereignty and independence of the individual governments.—The causes which have inspired a few men to assemble for very different purposes with such a degree of temerity as to break with a single stroke the union of America, and disseminate the seeds of discord through the land may be easily investigated, when we survey the partizans of monarchy in the state conventions, urging the adoption of a mode of government that militates with the former professions and exertions of this country, and with all ideas of republicanism, and the equal rights of men.

Passion, prejudice, and error, are characteristics of human nature; and as it cannot be accounted for on any principles of philosophy, religion, or good policy; to these shades in the human character must be attributed the mad zeal of some, to precipitate to a blind adoption of the measures of the late federal convention, without giving opportunity for better information to those who are misled by influence or ignorance into erroneous opinions. Literary talents may be prostituted, and the powers of genius debased to subserve the purposes of ambition or avarice; but the feelings of the heart will dictate the language of truth, and the simplicity of her accents will proclaim the infamy of those, who betray the rights of the people, under the specious, and popular pretence of *justice, consolidation, and dignity.*

It is presumed the great body of the people unite in sentiment with the writer of these observations, who most devoutly prays that public credit may rear her declining head, and remunerative justice pervade the land; nor is there a doubt if a free government is continued, that time and industry will enable both the public and private debtor to liquidate their arrearages in the most equitable manner. They wish to see the Confederated States bound together by the most indissoluble union, but without renouncing their separate sovereignties and independence, and becoming tributaries to a consolidated fabrick of aristocratick tyranny.—They wish to see government established, and peaceably holding the reins with honour, energy, and dignity; but they wish for no *federal city* whose *"cloud cap't towers"* may screen the state culprit from the hand of justice; while its exclusive jurisdiction may protect the riot of armies encamped within its limits.—They deprecate discord and civil convulsions, but they are not yet generally prepared with the ungrateful Israelites to ask a King, nor are their spirits sufficiently broken to yield the best of their olive grounds to his servants, and to see their sons appointed to run before his chariots—It has been observed by a zealous advocate for the new system, that most governments are the result of fraud or violence, and this with design to recommend its acceptance—but has not almost every step towards its fabrication been fraudulent in the extreme? Did not the prohibition strictly enjoined by the general

Convention, that no member should make any communication to his Constituents, or to gentlemen of consideration and abilities in the other States, bear evident marks of fraudulent designs?—This circumstance is regretted in strong terms by Mr. Martin, a member from Maryland, who acknowledges "He had no idea that all the wisdom, integrity, and virtue of the States was contained in that Convention, and that he wished to have corresponded with gentlemen of eminent political characters abroad, and to give their sentiments due weight"—he adds, "so extremely solicitous were they, that their proceedings should not transpire, that the members were prohibited from taking copies of their resolutions, or extracts from the Journals, without express permission, by vote."—And the hurry with which it has been urged to the acceptance of the people, without giving time, by adjournments, for better information, and more unanimity has a deceptive appearance; and if finally driven to resistance, as the only alternative between that and servitude, till in the confusion of discord, the reins should be seized by the violence of some enterprizing genius, that may sweep down the last barrier of liberty, it must be added to the score of criminality with which the fraudulent usurpation at Philadelphia, may be chargeable.—Heaven avert such a tremendous scene! and let us still hope a more happy termination of the present ferment:— may the people be calm and wait a legal redress; may the mad transport of some of our infatuated capitals subside; and every influential character through the States, make the most prudent exertions for a new general Convention, who may vest adequate powers in Congress, for all national purposes, without annihilating the individual governments, and drawing blood from every pore by taxes, impositions and illegal restrictions.—This step might again re-establish the Union, restore tranquility to the ruffled mind of the inhabitants, and save America from the distresses, dreadful even in contemplation.—"The great art of governing is to lay aside all prejudices and attachments to particular opinions, classes or individual characters to consult the spirit of the people; to give way to it; and in so doing, to give it a turn capable of inspiring those sentiments, which may induce them to relish a change, which an alteration of circumstances may hereafter make necessary."— The education of the advocates for monarchy should have taught them, and their memory should have suggested that "monarchy is a species of government fit only for a people too much corrupted by luxury, avarice, and a passion for pleasure, to have any love for their country, and whose vices the fear of punishment alone is able to restrain; but by no means calculated for a nation that is poor, and at the same time tenacious of their liberty—animated with a disgust to tyranny—and inspired with the generous feeling of patriotism and liberty, and at the same time, like the ancient Spartans have been hardened by temperance arid manly exertions, and equally despising the fatigues of the field, and the fear of enemies,"—and while they change their ground they should recollect, that Aristocracy is a still more formidable foe to public virtue, and the prosperity of a nation— that under such a government her patriots become mercenaries—her soldiers cowards, and the people slaves.—Though several State Conventions have assented to, and ratified, yet the voice of the people appears at present strong against the adoption of the Constitution.—By the chicanery, intrigue, and false colouring of those who plume themselves, more on their education and abilities, than their political, patriotic, or private virtues—the imbecility of some, and the duplicity of others, a majority of the Convention of Massachusetts have been flattered with the ideas of amendments, when it will be too late to complain—While several very worthy characters, too timid for their situation, magnified the hopeless alternative, between the dissolution of the bands of all government, and receiving the proffered system *in toto*, after long endeavouring to reconcile it to their consciences, swallowed the indigestible panacea, and in a kind of sudden desperation lent their signature to the dereliction of the honourable station they held in the Union, and have broken over the solemn compact, by which they were bound to support their own excellent constitution till the period of revision.—Yet Virginia, equally large and respectable, and who have done honour to themselves, by their vigorous exertions from the first dawn of independence, have not yet acted upon the question; they have wisely taken time to consider before they introduce innovations of a most dangerous nature: her inhabitants are brave, her burgesses are free, and they have a Governor who dares to think for himself, and to speak his opinion (without first pouring libations on the altar of popularity) though it should militate with some of the most accomplished and illustrious characters.

Maryland, who has no local interest to lead her to adopt, will doubtless reject the system—I hope the same characters still live, and that the same spirit which dictated to them a wise and cautious care, against sudden revolutions in government, and made them the last State that acceded to the independence of America, will lead them to support what they so deliberately claimed.—Georgia apprehensive of a war with the Savages, has acceded in order to insure protection.—Pennsylvania has struggled through much in the same manner, as the Massachusetts, against the manly feelings, and the masterly reasonings of a very respectable part of the Convention: They have adopted the system, and seen some of its authors burnt in effigy—their towns thrown into riot and confusion, and the minds of the people agitated by apprehension and discord.

New-Jersey and Delaware have united in the measure, from the locality of their situation, and the selfish motives which too generally govern mankind; the Federal City, and the seat of government, will naturally attract the intercourse of strangers—the youth of enterprize, and the wealth of the nation to the to the central States.

Connecticut has pushed it through with the precipitation of her neighbour, with few dissentient voices;—but more from irritation and resentment to a sister State, perhaps partiality to herself in her commercial regulations, than from a comprehensive view of the system, as a regard to the welfare of all.—But New York has motives, that will undoubtedly lead her to rejection, without being afraid to appeal to the understanding of mankind, to justify the grounds of their refusal to adopt a Constitution, that even the framers dare not to risque to the hazard of revision, amendment, or reconsideration, least the whole superstructure should be demolished by more skillful and discreet architects. I know not what part the Carolinas will take; but I hope their determinations will comport with the dignity and freedom of this country—their decisions will have great weight in the scale. But equally important are the small States of New Hampshire and Rhode Island:—New York, the Carolinas, Virginia, Maryland, and these two lesser States may yet support the liberties of the Continent; if they refuse a ratification, or postpone their proceedings till the spirits of the community have time to cool, there is little doubt but the wise measure of another federal convention will be adopted, when the members would have the advantage of viewing, at large, through the medium of truth, the objections that have been made from various quarters; such a measure might be attended with the most salutary effects, and prevent the dread consequences of civil feuds. But even if some of those large states should hastily accede, yet we have frequently seen in the story of revolution, relief spring from a quarter least expected.

Though the virtues of a Cato could not save Rome, nor the abilities of a Padilla defend the citizens of Castile from falling under the yoke of Charles; yet a *Tell* once suddenly rose from a little obscure city, and boldly rescued the liberties of his country.—Every age has its Bruti and its Decii, as well as its Caesars and Sejani:—The happiness of mankind depend much on the modes of government, and the virtues of the governors; and America may yet produce characters who have genius and capacity sufficient to form the manners and correct the morals of the people, and virtue enough to lead their country to freedom. Since their dismemberment from the British empire, America has, in many instances, resembled the conduct of a restless, vigorous, luxurious youth, prematurely emancipated from the authority of a parent, but without the experience necessary to direct him to act with dignity or discretion. Thus we have seen her break the shackles of foreign dominion, and all the blessings of peace restored on the more honourable terms: She acquired the liberty of framing her own laws, choosing her own magistrates, and adopting manners and modes of government the most favourable to the freedom and happiness of society. But how little have we availed ourselves of these superior advantages: The glorious fabric of liberty successfully reared with so much labor an assiduity totters to the foundation, and may be blown away as the bubble of fancy by the rude breath of military combinations, and politicians of yesterday.

It is true this country lately armed in opposition to regal despotism—impoverished by the expences of a long war, and unable immediately to fulfil their public or private engagements that appeared in some instances, with a boldness of spirit that seemed to set at defiance all authority, government, order, on the one hand; while on the other, there has been, not only a secret wish, but an open avowal of the necessity drawing the reins of government much too taught, not on. for a republicanism, but for a wise and limited monarchy.—But the character of this people is not averse to a degree subordination, the truth of this appears from the easy restoration of tranquility, after a dangerous insurrection in one of the states; this also evinces a little necessity of a complete revolution of government throughout the union. But it is a republican principle that the majority should rule; and if a spirit moderation should be cultivated on both sides, till the voice of the people at large could be fairly heard it should be held sacred.—And if, on such a scrutiny, the proposed constitution should appear repugnant to their character and wishes; if they, in the language of a late elegant pen, should acknowledge that "no confusion in my mind, is more terrible to them than the stern disciplined regularity and vaunted police of arbitrary governments, where every heart is depraved by fear, where mankind dare not assume their natural characters, where the free spirit must crouch to the slave in office, where genius must repress her effusions, or like the Egyptian worshippers, offer them in sacrifice to the calves in power, and where the human mind, always in shackles, shrinks from every generous effort." Who would then have the effrontery to say, it ought not to be thrown out with indignation, however some respectable names have appeared to support it.—But if after all, on a dispassionate and fair discussion, the people generally give their voices for a voluntary dereliction of their privileges, let every individual who chooses the active scenes of life strive to support the peace and unanimity of his country, though every other blessing may expire—And while the statesman is plodding for power, and the courtier practising the arts of dissimulation without check—while the rapacious are growing rich by oppression, and fortune throwing her gifts into the lap of fools, let the sublimer characters, the philosophic lovers of freedom who have wept over her exit, retire to the calm shades of contemplation, there they may look down with pity on the inconsistency of human nature, the revolutions of states; the rise of kingdoms, and the fall of empires.

DRAWING CONCLUSION:

1. What can we learn from this document about the concerns of anti-Federalists?

4.4 VIRGINIA CONVENTION RECOMMENDS AMENDMENTS TO THE CONSTITUTION (1788)

In Virginia, opposition to the proposed constitution was strong, and ratification was by no means assured. Anti-Federalist delegates argued that approval should be withheld until a number of changes were made in the document. Federalists, however, were able to secure a majority vote at the Virginia convention by linking ratification to a set of recommendations for constitutional amendments to be considered at the initial meeting of the new Congress. The list of amendments suggested by the Virginia convention was quite extensive and was divided into two portions: (1) recommendations for amendments to create a Bill of Rights to be added to the document; and (2) recommendations for amendments that would make changes to the main body of the Constitution. Some of the recommended amendments were eventually incorporated into the Bill of Rights. Others were never acted on. As you read through this long list of proposed amendments, think about which recommended changes were eventually adopted and which were not. Where were Federalists and anti-Federalists able to find common ground? On what issues were Federalists unwilling to move in the direction of anti-Federalists?

GUIDING QUESTIONS:

1. What provisions did the Virginia anti-Federalists want included in the Bill of Rights?
2. What changes to the main body of the Constitution did the Virginia anti-Federalists request?

We the Delegates of the People of Virginia duly elected in pursuance of a recommendation from the General Assembly and now met in Convention having fully and freely investigated and discussed the proceedings of the Federal Convention and being prepared as well as the most mature deliberation hath enabled us to decide thereon Do in the name and in behalf of the People of Virginia declare and make known that the powers granted under the Constitution being derived from the People of the United States may be resumed by them whensoever the same shall be perverted to their injury or oppression and that every power not granted thereby remains with them and at their will: that therefore no right of any denomination can be cancelled abridged restrained or modified by the Congress by the Senate or House of Representatives acting in any Capacity by the President or any Department or Officer of the United States except in those instances in which power is given by the Constitution for those purposes: & that among other essential rights the liberty of Conscience and of the Press cannot be cancelled abridged restrained or modified by any authority of the United States. With these impressions with a solemn appeal to the Searcher of hearts for the purity of our intentions and under the conviction that whatsoever imperfections may exist in the Constitution ought rather to be examined in the mode prescribed therein than to bring the Union into danger by a delay with a hope of obtaining Amendments previous to the Ratification, We the said Delegates in the name and in behalf of the People of Virginia do by these presents assent to and ratify the Constitution

From *Documentary History of the Constitution of the United States*, vol. 2 (Washington, DC: Department of State, 1894), 145–146, 377–385.

recommended on the seventeenth day of September one thousand seven hundred and eighty seven by the Federal Convention for the Government of the United States hereby announcing to all those whom it may concern that the said Constitution is binding upon the said People according to an authentic Copy hereto annexed in the Words following;

We the People of the United States in order to form a more perfect Union, establish Justice, ensure domestic tranquility, provide for the common defence, promote the general welfare, and secure the blessings of liberty to ourselves and our posterity do ordain and establish this Constitution for the United States of America.

[List of proposed additions to the Constitution . . .]

That there be a Declaration or Bill of Rights asserting and securing from encroachment the essential and unalienable Rights of the People in some such manner as the following:

First, That there are certain natural rights of which men, when they form a social compact cannot deprive or divest their posterity, among which are the enjoyment of life and liberty, with the means of acquiring, possessing and protecting property, and pursuing and obtaining happiness and safety. Second, That all power is naturally vested in and consequently derived from the people; that Magistrates, therefore, are their trustees and agents and at all times amenable to them. Third, That Government ought to be instituted for the common benefit, protection and security of the People; and that the doctrine of non-resistance against arbitrary power and oppression is absurd slavish, and destructive of the good and happiness of mankind. Fourth, That no man or set of Men are entitled to exclusive or separate public emoluments or privileges from the community, but in Consideration of public services; which not being descendible, neither ought the offices of Magistrate, Legislator or Judge, or any other public office to be hereditary. Fifth, That the legislative, executive, and judiciary powers of Government should be separate and distinct, and that the members of the two first may be restrained from oppression by feeling and participating the public burthens, they should, at fixt periods be reduced to a private station, return into the mass of the people; and the vacancies be supplied

by certain and regular elections; in which all or any part of the former members to be eligible or ineligible, as the rules of the Constitution of Government, and the laws shall direct. Sixth, That elections of representatives in the legislature ought to be free and frequent, and all men having sufficient evidence of permanent common interest with and attachment to the Community ought to have the right of suffrage: and no aid, charge, tax or fee can be set, rated, or levied upon the people without their own consent, or that of their representatives so elected, nor can they be bound by any law to which they have not in like manner assented for the public good. Seventh, That all power of suspending laws or the execution of laws by any authority, without the consent of the representatives of the people in the legislature is injurious to their rights, and ought not to be exercised. Eighth, That in all capital and criminal prosecutions, a man hath a right to demand the cause and nature of his accusation, to be confronted with the accusers and witnesses, to call for evidence and be allowed counsel in his favor, and to a fair and speedy trial by an impartial Jury of his vicinage, without whose unanimous consent he cannot be found guilty, (except in the government of the land and naval forces) nor can he be compelled to give evidence against himself. Ninth. That no freeman ought to be taken, imprisoned, or disseised of his freehold, liberties, privileges or franchises, or outlawed or exiled, or in any manner destroyed or deprived of his life, liberty or property but by the law of the land. Tenth. That every freeman restrained of his liberty is entitled to a remedy to enquire into the lawfulness thereof, and to remove the same, if unlawful, and that such remedy ought not to be denied nor delayed. Eleventh. That in controversies respecting property, and in suits between man and man, the ancient trial by Jury is one of the greatest Securities to the rights of the people, and ought to remain sacred and inviolable. Twelfth. That every freeman ought to find a certain remedy by recourse to the laws for all injuries and wrongs he may receive in his person, property or character. He ought to obtain right and justice freely without sale, compleatly and without denial, promptly and without delay, and that all establishments or regulations contravening these rights, are oppressive and unjust. Thirteenth, That excessive Bail ought not be required, nor excessive fines imposed, nor cruel and unusual punishments inflicted. Fourteenth, That every freeman has a right to be secure from all unreasonable searches and siezures of his person, his papers and his property; all warrants, therefore, to search suspected places, or sieze any freeman, his papers or property, without information upon Oath (or affirmation of a person religiously scrupulous of taking an oath) of legal and sufficient cause, are grievous and oppressive; and all general Warrants to search suspected places, or to apprehend any suspected person, without specially naming or describing the place or person, are dangerous and ought not to be granted. Fifteenth, That the people have a right peaceably to assemble together to consult for the common good, or to instruct their Representatives; and that every freeman has a right to petition or apply to the legislature for redress of grievances. Sixteenth, That the people have a right to freedom of speech, and of writing and publishing their Sentiments; but the freedom of the press is one of the greatest bulwarks of liberty and ought not to be violated. Seventeenth, That the people have a right to keep and bear arms; that a well regulated Militia composed of the body of the people trained to arms is the proper, natural and safe defence of a free State. That standing armies in time of peace are dangerous to liberty, and therefore ought to be avoided, as far as the circumstances and protection of the Community will admit; and that in all cases the military should be under strict subordination to and governed by the Civil power. Eighteenth, That no Soldier in time of peace ought to be quartered in any house without the consent of the owner, and in time of war in such manner only as the laws direct. Nineteenth, That any person religiously scrupulous of bearing arms ought to be exempted upon payment of an equivalent to employ another to bear arms in his stead. Twentieth, That religion or the duty which we owe to our Creator, and the manner of discharging it can be directed only by reason and conviction, not by force or violence, and therefore all men have an equal, natural and unalienable right to the free exercise of religion according to the dictates of conscience, and that no particular religious sect or society ought to be favored or established by Law in preference to others.

[List of proposed changes to the body of the Constitution . . .]

AMENDMENTS TO THE BODY OF THE CONSTITUTION

First, That each State in the Union shall respectively retain every power, jurisdiction and right which is not by this Constitution delegated to the Congress of the United States or to the departments of the Federal Government. Second, That there shall be one representative for every thirty thousand, according to the Enumeration or Census mentioned in the Constitution, until the whole number of representatives amounts to two hundred; after which that number shall be continued or encreased as the Congress shall direct, upon the principles fixed by the Constitution by apportioning the Representatives of each State to some greater number of people from time to time as population encreases. Third, When Congress shall lay direct taxes or excises, they shall immediately inform the Executive power of each State of the quota of such state according to the Census herein directed, which is proposed to be thereby raised; And if the Legislature of any State shall pass a law which shall be effectual for raising such quota at the time required by Congress, the taxes and excises laid by Congress shall not be collected, in such State. Fourth, That the members of the Senate and House of Representatives shall be ineligible to, and incapable of holding, any civil office under the authority of the United States, during the time for which they shall respectively be elected. Fifth, That the Journals of the proceedings of the Senate and House of Representatives shall be published at least once in every year, except such parts thereof relating to treaties, alliances or military operations, as in their judgment require secrecy. Sixth, That a regular statement and account of the receipts and expenditures of all public money shall be published at least once in every year. Seventh, That no commercial treaty shall be ratified without the concurrence of two thirds of the whole number of the members of the Senate; and no Treaty ceding, contracting, restraining or suspending the territorial rights or claims of the United States, or any of them or their, or any of their rights or claims to fishing in the American seas, or navigating the American rivers shall be but in cases of the most urgent and extreme necessity, nor shall any such treaty be ratified without the concurrence of three fourths of the whole number of the members of both houses respectively. Eighth, That no navigation law, or law regulating Commerce shall be passed without the consent of two thirds of the Members present in both houses. Ninth, That no standing army or regular troops shall be raised or kept up in time of peace, without the consent of two thirds of the members present in both houses. Tenth, That no soldier shall be inlisted for any longer term than four years, except in time of war, and then for no longer term than the continuance of the war. Eleventh, That each State respectively shall have the power to provide for organizing, arming and disciplining its own Militia, whensoever Congress shall omit or neglect to provide for the same. That the Militia shall not be subject to Martial law, except when in actual service in time of war, invasion, or rebellion; and when not in the actual service of the United States, shall be subject only to such fines, penalties and punishments as shall be directed or inflicted by the laws of its own State. Twelfth That the exclusive power of legislation given to Congress over the Federal Town and its adjacent District and other places purchased or to be purchased by Congress of any of the States shall extend only to such regulations as respect the police and good government thereof. Thirteenth, That no person shall be capable of being President of the United States for more than eight years in any term of sixteen years. Fourteenth, That the judicial power of the United States shall be vested in one supreme Court, and in such courts of Admiralty as Congress may from time to time ordain and establish in any of the different States: The Judicial power shall extend to all cases in Law and Equity arising under treaties made, or which shall be made under the authority of the United States; to all cases affecting ambassadors other foreign ministers and consuls; to all cases of Admiralty and maritime jurisdiction; to controversies to which the United States shall be a party; to controversies between two or [more] States, and between parties claiming lands under the grants of different States. In all cases affecting ambassadors, other foreign ministers and Consuls, and those in which a State shall be a party, the supreme court shall have original jurisdiction; in all other cases before mentioned the supreme Court shall have appellate jurisdiction as to matters of law only: except in cases of equity, and of admiralty and maritime jurisdiction, in which the Supreme Court shall have appellate jurisdiction both as to law and fact, with such exceptions and under such regulations as the Congress shall make. But the judicial power of the United States shall extend to no case where the cause of action shall have originated before the ratification of this Constitution; except in disputes between States about their Territory, disputes between persons claiming lands under the grants of different States, and suits for debts due to the United States. Fifteenth, That in criminal prosecutions no man shall be restrained in the exercise of the usual and accustomed right of challenging or excepting to the Jury. Sixteenth, That Congress shall not alter, modify or interfere in the times, places, or manner of holding elections for Senators and Representatives or either of them, except when the legislature of any State shall neglect, refuse or be disabled by invasion or rebellion to prescribe the same. Seventeenth, That those clauses which declare that Congress shall not exercise certain powers be not interpreted in any manner whatsoever to extend the powers of Congress. But that they may be construed either as making exceptions to the specified powers where this shall be the case, or otherwise as inserted merely for greater caution. Eighteenth, That the laws ascertaining the compensation to Senators and Representatives for their services be postponed in their operation, until after the election of Representatives immediately succeeding the passing thereof; that excepted, which shall first be passed on the Subject. Nineteenth, That some Tribunal other than the Senate be provided for trying impeachments of Senators. Twentieth, That the Salary of a Judge shall not be encreased or diminished during his continuance in Office, otherwise than by general regulations of Salary which may take place on a revision of the subject at stated periods of not less than seven years to commence from the time such Salaries shall be first ascertained by Congress. And the Convention do, in the name and behalf of the People of this Commonwealth enjoin it upon their Representatives in Congress to exert all their influence and use all reasonable and legal methods to obtain a Ratification of the foregoing alterations and provisions in the manner provided by the fifth article of the said Constitution; and in all Congressional laws to be passed in the mean time, to conform to the spirit of those Amendments as far as the said Constitution will admit.

Done in Convention this twenty seventh day of June in the year of our Lord one thousand seven hundred and eighty eight.

By order of the Convention.

EDMD PENDLETON President [SEAL.]

DRAWING CONCLUSIONS:

1. Which of the amendments proposed by the Virginia anti-Federalists were eventually adopted? Which were not?
2. What does this suggest about the types of issues on which Federalists and anti-Federalists could find common ground? On what type of issues could they not find common ground?

VOTING RESTRICTIONS AND SLAVE LAWS IN THE THIRTEEN ORIGINAL STATES

These charts provide information regarding voting restrictions and slave laws in the original thirteen states. The Constitution was almost entirely silent on the issue of who could or could not vote—voting restrictions were determined by state law instead of by the Constitution. The voting restrictions listed in the first chart were not required by the Constitution, but neither were they prohibited by it.

TABLE 1. VOTING RESTRICTIONS IN THE THIRTEEN ORIGINAL STATES

	Property Restrictions 1776	Property Restrictions Eliminated	Racial Restrictions 1776*	Racial Restrictions Added	Gender Restrictions 1776
New Hampshire	Yes	1784	No	-	Yes
Massachusetts	Yes	1821	No	-	Yes
Rhode Island	Yes	1842	No	-	Yes
Connecticut	Yes	1817	No	1818	Yes
New York	Yes	1821	No	1821**	Yes
New Jersey	Yes	1844	No	1807	No***
Pennsylvania	Yes	1776	No	1838	Yes
Delaware	Yes	1792	No	1792	Yes
Maryland	Yes	1810	No	1801	Yes
Virginia	Yes	1850	Yes	Already in Place	Yes
North Carolina	Yes	1854	No	1835	Yes
South Carolina	Yes	1810	No	1790	Yes
Georgia	Yes	1789	No	1777	Yes

* The absence of a racial restriction does not mean that all (or even most) black men could vote in a given state. Property restrictions barred all those who were enslaved (and many who were not) from voting.
** New York's 1821 constitution removed property restrictions for white men while retaining them for black men.
*** New Jersey allowed property owning women (who were very few in number) to vote until 1807.

The Constitution did contain a number of provisions regarding slavery (though the word "slave" was never used.) Article I, Section 2 declared that each state would receive a number of seats in the House of Representatives proportional to its free population plus 3/5ths of its slave population. Article I, Section 9 barred Congress from banning the importation of slaves until the year 1808. Article IV, Section 2 required escaped slaves who crossed state lines to be returned to their masters regardless of whether slavery was legal in the state to which they escaped. In addition, Amendment V's protections for private property could be interpreted as denying Congress the power to outlaw slavery. Like voting restrictions, however, the existence of slavery was determined not by the Constitution but by state law. The slave laws listed in the second chart (Table 2) were neither required by the Constitution nor prohibited by it.

TABLE 2. SLAVERY AND ABOLITION IN THE THIRTEEN ORIGINAL STATES

	Slavery Legal 1776	Date Slavery Abolished*	Immediate or Gradual
New Hampshire	Yes	1790–1810**	?
Massachusetts	Yes	1783***	Immediate
Rhode Island	Yes	1784	Gradual
Connecticut	Yes	1784	Gradual
New York	Yes	1799	Gradual
New Jersey	Yes	1804	Gradual
Pennsylvania	Yes	1780	Gradual
Delaware	Yes	-	
Maryland	Yes	-	
Virginia	Yes	-	
North Carolina	Yes	-	
South Carolina	Yes	-	
Georgia	Yes	-	

* Excludes those states where slavery was abolished by the 13th Amendment to the Constitution, ratified in 1865 at the conclusion of the Civil War.

** New Hampshire's 1783 state constitution declared that "all men are born equal and independent." While there is no evidence of a specific piece of legislation or court ruling abolishing slavery, by 1810 the federal census indicated a complete absence of slaves in New Hampshire.

*** In 1783 the Massachusetts Supreme Court found that a clause in the 1780 state constitution declaring "all men are born free and equal" to be inconsistent with slavery.

BIOGRAPHIES OF KEY FEDERALISTS

When seeking to determine the motives of the individuals who created the Constitution of the United States, it is useful to know something about them as individuals. Alexander Hamilton and James Madison were two of the key architects of the Constitution. They each played an instrumental role in convening the Constitutional Convention of 1787. While Hamilton's influence on the actual work of the convention was limited, Madison was its single most influential member. Writing under the pseudonym "Publius," the pair (along with colleague John Jay) collaborated on a series of essays (later dubbed the "Federalist Papers") that proved pivotal in the successful campaign for ratification of the Constitution. As you read these brief biographies of Hamilton and Madison, look for information about their personal, professional, and political lives that might shed some light on the reasons why they became so devoted to the cause of replacing the Articles of Confederation with a constitution that shifted power from the states to the federal government.

GUIDING QUESTIONS:

1. What were the family and educational backgrounds of Hamilton and Madison?
2. What role did each play in the American Revolution?
3. What were the professional backgrounds of Hamilton and Madison?
4. What was the nature of their involvement in politics prior the convening of the Constitutional Convention? What types of issues had they each concerned themselves with?

6.1 ALEXANDER HAMILTON

Alexander Hamilton's life was a classic rags to riches story. Born out of wedlock in the 1750s in the British colonies of the West Indies (his exact birthdate is unknown), his father abandoned him at a young age and his mother (who had supported Alexander and his brother by keeping a small store on the island of St. Croix) died of yellow fever a few years later. The young Hamilton obtained employment as a clerk in a local merchant house, where he impressed his employers will his skills and his ambition. An avid reader, Hamilton took great pains to educate himself. In 1772, a group of local community leaders raised the funds needed for Hamilton to pursue his formal education in the British colonies on the North American mainland.

In the fall of 1773, Hamilton enrolled in King's College (now Columbia University) in New York City. His attention, however, was soon drawn to the growing Patriot movement. In 1774 and 1775, he published a series of tracts and articles condemning the policies of the British Empire toward the colonies and supporting the colonial resistance. With the outbreak of hostilities in 1775, Hamilton joined a volunteer militia company in New York. The next year he organized an artillery company for George Washington's Continental Army and received a commission as captain. Hamilton saw combat in a series of engagements, including the revolutionary victory at the Battle of Princeton in January of 1777.

Hamilton's true talent, though, lay less with command than with administration. In 1777, he accepted an invitation to serve as aide to General Washington and was promoted to lieutenant colonel. As Washington's aide, his duties included political relations with the Continental Congress and the governors of the various states, diplomacy with foreign nations, and negotiations with other high-ranking military officers. It was during this time that Hamilton developed his lifelong interest in government finance, as the Congress struggled to raise the funds needed to supply and furnish the Continental Army. It was also during this time that Hamilton's frustrations with the system of government established by the Articles of Confederation first became apparent, as did his dislike for those that he considered to be posturing politicians.

In 1780, Hamilton married Elizabeth Schuyler, the daughter of a wealthy New York landowning family, a move that cemented Hamilton's position within the state's economic and social elite. Following the great revolutionary victory at Yorktown (the battle that essentially ended the war), Hamilton resigned his commission in the army and took up family life. In 1782, he passed the New York bar exam and pursued a career in law, becoming one of New York City's most prominent attorneys. Despite his successful legal career, he nonetheless retained his interest in public life. In 1782, New York's legislature selected Hamilton as a representative to the Continental Congress, where he devoted much of his time and energy to seeking a reliable source of revenue for the national government. Frustrated with the failure of Congress to find a solution to the problem of government finance, Hamilton joined forces with James Madison of Virginia to organize the Philadelphia Convention of 1787, where the new federal constitution was framed. While Hamilton's influence among the convention delegates was limited—his proposal for the President and members of the Senate to serve for life, for instance, was rejected—he played a pivotal role in the successful campaign to secure ratification of the proposed constitution.

In 1789, newly elected president George Washington asked Hamilton to serve as the nation's first Secretary of the Treasury. From that position, Hamilton worked to put in place the foundations of a modern system of banking and finance for the newly independent United States. In recognition of this work, Hamilton's face graces the front of the ten dollar bill, the only non-president to appear on US currency. Hamilton died in an 1804 duel at the hands of Vice President Aaron Burr, a political rival.

6.2 JAMES MADISON

James Madison, often considered the "father of the US Constitution," had a greater influence on the document adopted at the Philadelphia convention of 1787 than did any other individual. A son of the slave South, Madison was born into a wealthy Virginia landowning and slave-owning family. At the time, it was common for the sons of the plantation elite to receive a classical education that included the study of such subjects as philosophy, mathematics, geography, theology, and Greek and Latin languages. Between the ages of eleven and sixteen, Madison attended a Virginia boarding school. After receiving two years of college-preparatory tutoring at home, Madison enrolled at the College of New Jersey (today's Princeton University) in 1769. Colonial protests against the taxation policies of the British Empire had been underway for several years, and the College of New Jersey was a hotbed of patriotic sentiment. John Witherspoon, the college president, was a fierce critic of British policies who went on to become a prominent revolutionary leader and a signatory of the Declaration of Independence. Students at the college participated actively in the growing colonial resistance movement, and Madison became a supporter of the cause. Upon completing his studies in 1772, he returned home to Virginia and took up management of the family's plantation.

As the confrontation between the colonists and the British Empire veered toward open conflict, Madison devoted increased energy to revolutionary activities. In 1774, he joined his county's Committee of Safety, a group charged with making local military preparations in anticipation of war. Poor health, however, prevented Madison from serving in the military. Instead, he pursued the role of revolutionary political leader. In 1776, he was elected as a delegate to the convention at which Virginia declared its independence from Britain and adopted its own state constitution. At the convention, Madison fought successfully to ensure that the constitution included strong protections for religious liberty. Between 1777 and 1779, he served on Virginia's Council of State, an executive body that worked in conjunction with the state's governor to oversee day-to-day government operations, including military operations. In 1779, the state legislature chose Madison to represent Virginia in the Continental Congress, a role he filled until 1783. Between 1784 and 1786 he served in Virginia's legislature where his accomplishments included orchestrating the adoption of the state's landmark Statute for Religious Freedom (authored by Madison's friend and colleague Thomas Jefferson).

As a member of Congress and as a member of the Virginia state legislature, Madison pushed unsuccessfully for a series of amendments to the Articles of Confederation that would have strengthened congressional powers. One proposal, for instance, would have provided Congress with an independent source of revenue through a tax on foreign imports. A second would have allowed Congress to impose retaliatory tariffs in response to foreign restrictions on the export of American goods. Madison's frustrations with the system of government established by the Articles were exacerbated by the tendency of the states to enact what he saw as unjust laws. "The general rage for paper money," as Madison termed it, especially drew his ire. Though it was a popular debt relief measure, Madison considered the issuing of large amounts of paper money to be an assault on private property, and he described it as an "epidemic malady."

Madison played an instrumental role in the convening of the 1787 constitutional convention and was a primary author of the Virginia Plan that served as an outline for the proposed constitution that the convention ultimately adopted. During the constitutional ratification process, Madison resisted calls for the addition of a bill of rights. To secure approval of the constitution, however, Federalists like Madison were forced to promise that a bill of rights would be adopted. Elected to the newly constituted House of Representatives in 1789, Madison took the lead in developing the series of constitutional amendments that became the federal Bill of Rights. Madison went on to a long and distinguished public career that included service as the country's Secretary of State under President Thomas Jefferson and two terms as president himself. He died in 1836 at his plantation home of Montpelier at the age of eighty-five.

DRAWING CONCLUSION:

1. What aspects of the personal, professional, and political lives of Hamilton and Madison might it be important to keep in mind when seeking to determine their motives for seeking a shift in power from the states to the federal government?

ADDITIONAL RESOURCES

Beard, Charles A. *An Economic Interpretation of the Constitution of the United States*. New York: The Macmillan Company, 1913.

Beeman, Richard. *Plain and Honest Men: The Making of the American Constitution*. New York: Random House, 2009.

Berkin, Carol. *A Brilliant Solution: Inventing the American Constitution*. New York: Harcourt, 2002.

Diamond, Martin. *The Founding of the Democratic Republic*. Itasca, IL: F.E. Peacock Publishers, 1981.

Finkelman, Paul. *Slavery and the Founders: Race and Liberty in the Age of Jefferson*. Armonk, NY: M. E. Sharpe, 1996.

Gibson, Alan. *Interpreting the Founding: Guide to the Enduring Debates over the Origins and Foundations of the American Republic*. Lawrence: University of Kansas Press, 2006.

Goldwin, Robert A. and William A. Schambra, eds. *How Democratic Is the Constitution?* Washington, DC: American Enterprise Institute for Public Policy Research, 1980.

Holton, Woody. *Unruly Americans and the Origins of the Constitution*. New York: Hill and Wang, 2007.

Kerber, Linda. *Women of the Republic: Intellect and Ideology in Revolutionary America*. Chapel Hill: University of North Carolina Press, 1980.

McDonald, Forrest. *E Pluribus Unum: The Formation of the American Republic, 1776–1790*. Boston, MA: Houghton Mifflin Company, 1965.

McDonald, Forrest. *We the People: The Economic Origins of the Constitution*. Chicago: The University of Chicago Press, 1958.

Shankman, Andrew. *Original Intents: Hamilton, Jefferson, Madison, and the American Founding*. New York: Oxford University Press, 2018.

Tise, Larry E. *The American Counterrevolution: A Retreat from Liberty, 1783–1800*. Mechanicsburg, PA: Stackpole Books, 1998.

Wood, Gordon S. *The Radicalism of the American Revolution*. New York: Alfred A Knopf, 1992.

INDEX

Note: In this index, *T* indicates a reference to the Timeline while *t* indicates a table.

A

amendments. *See also* Bill of Rights
  to Articles of Confederation, 4
    in Constitution, 46
    in Philadelphia Convention, 16
    Virginia Convention, 101–105
American Revolution
    democratic tendencies unleashed, 15, 19, 20, 30
    Hamilton's role, 109
    Madison's role, 110
    overview of, 19
    veteran activism, 20
    Warren on, 91
Annapolis Convention, 4
Anti-Federalists
    absence of bill of rights, 17, 61
    documents, 85–100
    major concerns summarized, 17
    Montezuma essay, 86–88
    "Political Creed of Every Federalist," 89
    Mercy Owen Warren essay, 90–100
appointments
    Madison on, 78–79
    Montezuma essay on, 86
    Pennsylvania Constitution, 57
aristocracy
    American Revolution and, 19, 20
    colonial administration, 20
    Constitution as aristocratic document, 6
    as foe of public virtue, 98
    satiric view of, 89
    Warren on, 91–92, 97, 98

arms, right to bear
    Bill of Rights, 61
    Pennsylvania Constitution, 54
    Virginia Convention, 103
Articles of Confederation, 3. *See also* Timeline
    concerns of Philadelphia delegates, 3
    Confederation Congress, 21
    decision making rules, 45
    efforts to amend, 4
    "league of friendship" among states, 33, 34
    Madison on vices of the system, 70–73
    Madison's frustration with, 110
    proposal to replace, 5–6
    selection of representatives, 34
    text of, 33–38
    vision of, 3
    weaknesses, 3–4, 15–16
artisans, 20
assembly, right to peaceable
    Bill of Rights, 61
    Pennsylvania Constitution, 54
    Virginia Convention, 103

B

bail, excessive
    Bill of Rights, 62
    Pennsylvania Constitution, 58
    Virginia Constitution, 48
    Virginia Convention, 103
Beard, Charles, 7, 23
Beeman, Richard, 18

Bill of Rights. *See also* Timeline
    added, 22
    Federalist promises, 6–7
    focus on individual rights, 61
    Madison's role, 17, 110–111
    originally absent, 6, 17, 22, 61
    Philadelphia Convention, 22
    text of, 61–62
    Virginia Convention, 102
    Warren on, 95
board member decisions, 66
Boston Tea Party, 15
boundary disputes, Hamilton on, 66
Burr, Aaron, 109

C

Canada, 37
centralized government
    challenge of, 16
    wariness of, 15
checks and balances
    Madison on, 78–81
    in Philadelphia Convention, 16
    Virginia Convention, 102
civil service
    need for, Hamilton on, 66
    public servants' compensation, 58
colonial governments, 20
Columbian Patriot (pen name). *See* Warren, Mercy Otis
Committee of the States, Articles of Confederation, 37
commoner political participation, after Revolution, 20–21
Common Sense (Paine), 19
Commonwealth of Pennsylvania, 55, 57
Commonwealth of Virginia, 51
Confederation Congress, 21
Congress, Hamilton on, 65–66
Constitution, Pennsylvania
    Declaration of the Rights of the Inhabitants, 53–59
    Oath or Affirmation of Allegiance, 59
    Oath or Affirmation of Office, 59–60
    supreme executive council, 56–57
    text of, 52–53
Constitution, U.S.
    amendments subsequent to, 22
    basic principles, 18
    complexity, 39
    as conspiracy of well-born against rabble, 86–88
    containing democracy, 19
    context of the times, 23
    Declaration of Independence compared, 23
    division of powers, 78
    flaws critiqued, 90–100
    limitations, overview of, 17
    limits on powers of state governments, 39
    Montezuma essay on, 86–88
    opposing views of, 23
    as perversion of state and individual rights, 95

    prejudices of founding fathers, 17
    proposal debated, 6
    as set of rules, 29, 39
    seven articles summarized, 39
    significance, 7
    on slavery, 25–26
    state constitutions compared, 47
    text of, 39–46
    three branches, 39
    Virginia Convention, 101–105
Constitution, Virginia
    Bill of Rights, 47–48
    right to suffrage, 47
    text of, 48–52
Continental Army, 20
    Hamilton in, 109
Continental Congress, 12
    Virginia delegates, 51
copyright law, 42
Council of Censors, Pennsylvania Constitution, 59–60
currency
    Articles of Confederation, 36
    in Constitution, 42
    value of, Madison on, 71

D

debtors, factions and, 76
debt prison, Pennsylvania Constitution, 58
debt relief for farmers. *See also* Timeline
    controversies, 4–5
    Hamilton on, 68–69
    Madison on, 71
    paper money, 3–4
    Shays' Rebellion, 83
Declaration of Independence
    as argument for independence, 30
    Constitution compared, 23
    equality, 19, 23
    principles at stake, 15
    text of, 30–32
    Warren citing, 92
democracy, republic compared, 76–77
democratic theory of government, 32
Demos, John, 24
despotism, Warren on, 91, 92, 93, 94, 97, 100
Diamond, Martin, 17, 23
division of powers, Virginia Convention, 102
Duane, James, 64

E

elections
    in Constitution, 41
    frequency, 93
    Madison on, 73
    Pennsylvania Constitution, 53, 54–55, 56, 58
    sheriffs and coroners, 58
    Virginia Constitution, 48

Virginia Convention, 102, 104
Warren on, 93
electoral college
in Constitution, 43, 44
in Philadelphia Convention, 16
Warren on, 95
elites
after Revolution, 20–21
Beard on, 7
fears after Revolution, 19
men of property for Hamilton, 68
emigration issue, from one state to another, 54
equality
Bill of Rights, 51
Constitution and, 29
eighteenth century assumptions versus, 23–24
Jefferson on, 23
Montezuma essay on, 86
Pennsylvania Constitution, 53
slavery and, 17
in thirteen colonies, 20
executive branch. *See also* President
in Constitution, 39, 43, 44
Warren on, 93

F
factions
causes of, 75
defining, 75
influence of factious leaders, 77
Madison on, 72, 73, 74–77
specific issues, 82
two methods of removing, 75
Federalist documents, 63
Hamilton essay on Constitution, 68–69
Hamilton letter to James Duane, 64–67
Madison on vices of the political system, 70–73
Madison's "Federalist No. 10," 74–77
Madison's "Federalist No. 51," 78–81
"Federalist No. 10" (Madison), 74–77
"Federalist No. 51" (Madison), 78–81
"Federalist Papers," significance, 74, 108
Federalists. *See also* Hamilton, Alexander; Madison, James
absence of bill of rights, 61
biographies, 108–111
concept of, 6
motives portrayed, 86–88
opposition to, 86
ratification, 17
satiric summary of views, 89
federal republic, Warren on, 93
federal system, Madison's
reflections on, 79–81
Federal Town, 104
fugitive slave law
Constitution, 26
in Constitution, 45

G
Germanic states, 66
governing, art of, 98
government, nature of, Madison on, 79
governors
after Revolution, 20
Virginia Constitution, 50
Gray, Daniel, 83
Great Britain
colonial governments, 20
colonist frustration with, 15
Declaration of Independence, 31–32
Hamilton on, 69
revolutionaries engaged in treason, 30
trade after Revolution, 21
trade blockade, 4
Virginia Constitution, 48–49, 52
Warren on, 91, 96–97
Grecian republics, 65
Grover, Thomas, 83

H
habeas corpus
in Constitution, 43
Montezuma essay on, 88
Shays' Rebellion, 83
Hamilton, Alexander
background, 4, 109
biography, 109
on central vs. state-level power, 4, 5
"Conjectures about the Constitution," 68–69
dangers of local politics, 5
on defects of Congress, 64–65
letter to James Duane, 64–67
Philadelphia Convention, 4, 21
as representative of the elite, 19, 21
Secretary of the Treasury, 109
significance, 108
on undefined powers, 65
households
basis of economic production, 24
centrality of, 24
consent of the governed, 25
role of heads of, 24, 26
social positions in, 24–25
as society's building blocks, 23
subordinated members, 24–25, 26
House of Representatives
in Constitution, 40
House of Delegates (Virginia), 49–50
Montezuma essay on, 86
Pennsylvania Constitution, 54, 55
Philadelphia Convention, 16, 21
Virginia Convention, 103
Warren on, 95
hunting and fishing rights, 59

I

immigration
 in Constitution, 43
 Pennsylvania Constitution, 59
impeachment
 in Constitution, 40
 Pennsylvania Constitution, 57
 of president and others, 44
 Senate powers, 41
 Virginia Constitution, 51
 Virginia Convention, 104
individual, emphasis on, 23
 Warren on, 95

J

Jay, John, 108
Jefferson, Thomas
 consent of the governed, 25
 Declaration of Independence, 30–32
 on equality, 23, 25
 Madison in cabinet, 111
 principles of legitimate government power, 30
judicial branch
 in Constitution, 39, 44–45
 Madison on, 78–79
 Montezuma essay on, 87–88
 Pennsylvania Constitution, 57–59
 Philadelphia Convention, 16, 22
 Virginia Constitution, 51
 Virginia Convention, 104
 Warren on, 93
jury trials
 Bill of Rights, 62
 in Constitution, 45
 Pennsylvania Constitution, 53, 57
 satiric view, 89
 Virginia Constitution, 48
 Virginia Convention, 102
 Warren on, 93–94
justices of the peace, Virginia Constitution, 51

L

legislative branch
 in Constitution, 39
 legal immunity of legislators, 41
 Madison on, 79
 Philadelphia Convention, 16, 21
 Warren on, 93
Lewis, Jan, 26
Lieutenant Governor, 50

M

Madison, James
 Bill of Rights, 17
 biography, 110–111
 on central versus state-level power, 4, 5
 dangers of local politics, 5
 "Federalist No. 51," 78–81

 as representative of the elite, 19
 significance, 108
 on vices of the political system, 70–73
majority versus minority issue. *See* minority versus majority
 issue
mankind, happiness of, 99
Maryland, on ratification, 98–99
Massachusetts
 amendments offered, 96, 98
 colonial rule, 96–97
 colonial structure, 24
 paper money, 5
 Shays' Rebellion, 5
 writs of assistance, 95
military
 satiric view, 88, 89
 standing armies issue, 89, 94
 Virginia Convention, 103
militia
 Articles of Confederation, 35
 Bill of Rights, 62
 civilian influence in, 65
 Hamilton on, 67
 Virginia Constitution, 48, 51
 Virginia Convention, 103, 104
 Warren on, 94
minority versus majority issue, 71
 factions, 76
 Madison on, 76, 80
monarchy
 nature of, 98
 secret wish for, 100
money, issuing,
 Philadelphia Convention, 22
Montezuma essay, 86–88
Morgan, Edmund, 17, 23

N

natural rights, 52
 Virginia Convention, 102
New Hampshire
 backgrounds of representatives, 20–21
 ratification high jinks, 6–7

O

Oath or Affirmation of Allegiance, Pennsylvania
 Constitution, 59
"Observations on the New Constitution, And on the Federal
 and State Conventions" (Warren), 90–100
officeholding
 in perpetuity, 86, 94
 Virginia Convention on, 102

P

Paine, Thomas, 19
paper money
 after Revolutionary War, 3–4, 21

debt relief for farmers, 4–5, 21
    Madison on, 71, 72, 110
    Massachusetts, 5
    Rhode Island, 5
Parenti, Michael, 19, 23
people/commoners
    critics of proposed constitution, 6
    satiric view of, 89
    Virginia Convention, 102
Philadelphia Convention of 1787, 3, 16. *See also* Timeline
    Federalist role, 108
    as fraudulent usurpation, 98
    goals of, 16, 21
    Hamilton's influence, 108, 109
    Madison on vices of the political system, 70–73
    Madison's influence, 108, 110
police forces
    Hamilton on, 65
    Pennsylvania Constitution, 53
    Shays' Rebellion, 83, 84
political parties, division of powers, 80
political philosophers, 15, 18
postal service, 42
power
    nature of, 88
    origin of, 92
    without limitations, and corruption, 93
President. *See also* executive branch
    powers of, 16
    powers seen by Montezuma essay, 87
    terms in Philadelphia Convention, 16
    Virginia Convention, 104
press, freedom of
    Bill of Rights, 61
    Montezuma essay on, 88
    Pennsylvania Constitution, 54
    satiric views, 88, 89
    Virginia Constitution, 48
    Virginia Convention, 101, 103
    Warren on, 93
privilege clause, 87
Privy Council, or Council of State (Virginia), 50
property ownership, 20
    factions related, 75, 76
    Pennsylvania Constitution, 54
property rights
    democratic spirit, Hamilton on, 68
    Madison on, 75
Publius (pen name), 74, 108
pure democracy, Madison on, 76

R

ratification. *See also* Timeline
    of amendments to Constitution, 46
    conventions, in Constitution, 46
    Hamilton on prospects for, 68
    method established, 6
    parody of pro-ratification forces, 89

    process unfolding, 6–7
    satire of pro-ratification arguments, 86–88
    Virginia Convention, 101–105
    Warren on, 92, 98–99
ratification conventions, 6
    Federalist and anti-Federalist battles, 17
    in Philadelphia Convention, 16
    Virginia recommending amendments, 101–105
    Warren on, 98–99
religion
    legislator oaths, 46
    Madison on, 72
    military exemption, 103
religion, freedom of
    Bill of Rights, 61
    civil rights and, 80
    Madison, 110
    Pennsylvania Constitution, 53
    Virginia Constitution, 48
    Virginia Convention, 103
representatives
    Madison on, 71–72
    Virginia Convention on, 103
republic, Madison defining, 76
republican government
    commitment to, 17
    in Constitution, 45
    Madison on, 74, 79
    political philosophers on, 15
    Warren on, 91, 92, 94
Rhode Island
    dangers of faction, 82
    Madison on, 80
    paper money, 5
Rules of Proceedings, 41

S

Schuyler, Elizabeth, 109
search and seizure, freedom from unlawful
    Bill of Rights, 62
    Pennsylvania Constitution, 53–54
    Virginia Constitution, 48
    Virginia Convention, 103
    Warren on, 95
Senate
    in Constitution, 41
    direct election of senators, 17
    members chosen by state legislature, 16
    terms in Philadelphia Convention, 16
    Virginia Constitution, 50
    Virginia Convention, 103
    Warren on, 95
Shays' Rebellion, 5, 16
    documents, 82–84
    elite view, 21
    Gray on grievances, 83–84
    Grover on grievances, 84
slaveholders, protection in Philadelphia Convention, 21

slave laws, thirteen original states, 107t
slavery
    abolition, 22
    in colonial household, 24–25
    Constitution's implicit recognition of, 17
    Madison on, 71
    at state level, 25–26
    three fifths formula, 40, 107
small versus larger republics, 74, 77, 80
society, principal aim of, 93
speech, freedom
    Articles of Confederation, 33
    Pennsylvania Constitution, 52
speech, freedom of
    Bill of Rights, 61
    Virginia Convention, 103
state constitutions
    after Revolution, 20
    Hamilton on, 65
state governments
    after American Revolution, 19, 20–21
    Articles of Confederation, 33–38
    in Constitution, 45
    critiques by Madison, 70–73, 110
    Hamilton and Madison on, 4, 108
    Hamilton on, 68
    limits on power of, 39, 43
    Montezuma essay on, 87
    powers under Bill of Rights, 62
    representatives democratized, 20–21
    Warren on, 96
State of the Union (address), 44
suffrage
    before Revolution, 4
    Constitution on, 25
    in household, 25
    Pennsylvania Constitution, 54, 60
    property restrictions, 20, 25, 47
    thirteen original states, 106t
    Virginia Constitution, 47, 50
    Virginia Convention, 102
Supreme Court
    Virginia Convention, 104
    Warren on, 95
Swiss cantons, 65–66

T
taxes
    Boston Tea Party, 15
    colonial protests, 110
    in Constitution, 40, 42, 43
    Hamilton on, 66
    Pennsylvania Constitution, 59
    Virginia Convention, 102, 103
    Warren on, 90, 94
territories
    admission of new states, 45
    Warren on, 95–96

three branches
    Madison on, 78–81
    U.S. Constitution, 39, 78
    Virginia Constitution, 49
    Virginia Convention, 102
trade
    Articles of Confederation, 4
    Madison critique of Articles of Confederation, 71
    Virginia Convention, 103
treason, in Constitution, 45
Treaty of Paris, 15
tyranny
    aristocratic, 97
    British government as, 15
    challenge of central government, 16
    fears expressed in Declaration of Independence,
        30–32
    Warren on, 91, 94, 97

V
veto, presidential, 16
    Philadelphia Convention, 22
Vice President,
    in Constitution, 41
Virginia
    black men barred from voting, 26
    borders, 52
    on ratification, 98–99
Virginia colony, 24
Virginia Constitution. See Constitution, Virginia
Virginia Convention, 105–106
Virginia Plan
    as framework for Philadelphia Convention, 6
    Madison's role, 110
voting rights.
    See suffrage

W
war and peace
    Articles of Confederation, 35, 37
    Bill of Rights, 62
    Commander in Chief, 44
    in Constitution, 42
    Hamilton on, 64
    Virginia Convention, 104
Warren, Mercy Otis, 90–100
Washington, George
    Continental Army, 20
    Hamilton as aide, 108
    Hamilton on, 68, 69
women
    in colonial household, 24–25
    legal rights, 25
    right to vote, 4, 26
    Mercy Otis Warren, 90–100
Wood, Gordon, 19